Jenny

THERESE SLUSHER

TRILOGY
A wholly owned subsidiary of TBN

Trilogy Christian Publishers
A Wholly Owned Subsidary of Trinity Broadcasting Network
2442 Michelle Drive
Tustin, CA 92780

For information, address Trilogy Christian Publishing
Rights Department, 2442 Michelle Drive, Tustin, Ca 92780.
Trilogy Christian Publishing/ TBN and colophon are trademarks of Trinity Broadcasting Network.

For information about special discounts for bulk purchases, please contact Trilogy Christian Publishing.

Manufactured in the United States of America

10 9 8 7 6 5 4 3 2 1

Library of Congress Cataloging-in-Publication Data is available.

ISBN 978-1-64773-098-7 (Print Book)
ISBN 978-1-64773-099-4 (ebook)

Her parents were killed on the mission field.
Will her faith survive another loss?

ACKNOWLEDGMENT

. . . .

TO MY MOM, YOU have always been my biggest cheerleader, travel companion, and fellow book lover. Thank you for being spontaneous and handing your phone to a complete stranger at a conference because meeting Sherri Downs set me on this path.

Thanks to all of my family and friends. My support network is something to behold. I have tried to honor one and all by sprinkling my characters with familiar names. This is my gift to all of you for your never-ending support. If you don't see yourself in book 1, just watch for it in book 2.

Thanks to my cousin Cathie for faithfully reading every single version of this book (and there were at least four). She loved them all, so she's a little biased, but I appreciated her enthusiasm.

And for my friend and editor, Ian, who got me over the finish line. He made this a better story and all of his changes made me a better writer.

MARGARET WOKE UP AND listened. The silence was deafening. Something was very wrong. The jungle was silent only when a predator was nearby or a storm was moving in. She moved slightly and shook her husband of twenty-eight years lightly on the shoulder. He opened his warm brown eyes and blinked. It took him only a moment to come fully awake. *He had always been like that,* she thought wryly. *Instantly alert, ready to go moments after waking.*

Margaret stumbled through mornings, looking for quiet time and coffee. She had always envied that morning quality in Jack.

Since coming to the jungle, that instant alertness had saved their lives on more than one occasion. The politics of the tribes that lay within the scope of their mission field often erupted into warfare. Raids on the camps were becoming more and more frequent. It was a volatile and dangerous situation that she and Jack had talked about and prayed about late into the nights. The chief of the tribe they had been assigned to, Moyabu, would send his son, Mato, at the first sign of trouble, and Jack would move into action immediately with no hesitations. He would get them out of the tent and the camp within minutes of being awakened by Mato.

Trouble must have come again. The jungle was never this quiet. This still. She sensed that they needed to get out even though Mato had not appeared. Jack responded to the silent question in her eyes, and they both scrambled quickly from their straw cot. Margaret's knees protested, but she shook off the signs of her age and kept going. They paused occasionally to look at each other as they went about gathering a backpack with supplies. They had been here before. They knew the drill. They both had assigned tasks: Margaret gathered the notebooks and the Bible; Jack grabbed the water and the flashlight. They moved around the tent in the dark with the ease of knowing where everything was.

Margaret was afraid, and that surprised her. She had not been afraid since the first few months here when the raids were new and unexpected. It had been such a departure from the sameness of their life in Alaska.

The raids back then were less frequent, but when they happened, Mato would come, bending over their cot and waking them not so much by his touch as by his presence. Her eyes would fly open to his dark unsmiling face, and her chest would constrict painfully, the adrenaline rush immediate. She thought she had made a mistake in coming at first, thought for sure she was going to have a heart attack.

After a raid, it would be days before she was calm enough to sleep again. Eventually, Mato became a comfort. He would wake them silently and nod for them to go. Then he would slip out silently back to his duties, back to the chief. He never spoke a word, and they learned to do likewise even a whisper carried in the jungle.

Where was he? Was it a false alarm? Things had been quiet for weeks. They had heard of no uprisings in the vicinity although the government frequently tried to mobilize the impoverished villages to fight.

Many homes in the villages a week's walk away from theirs had been destroyed by rebel shelling. They were deeper into the jungle than the other settlements and had been kept safer than most. The death squads roamed everywhere, looking to execute Abu Sayyaf suspects—enemies of the government. The unrest was a constant reminder to her of the tenuous thread one had on life.

She shifted the things in her arms feeling the wrongness of the moment. She moved to the back flap of the tent. Jack was right behind her. Margaret drew the zipper of the tent back, wincing at the sound. Small but if someone was nearby enough to give away their position.

Thoughts of Jenny and Todd came suddenly, but she pushed them away. No time to think of her kids. They had to get away. Jack tried to reassure her by placing his hand on her shoulder, reminding her in body language to go slow and to be careful. She wondered at the level of communication they now shared. They could almost read each other's thoughts, could understand each other's body language as if speaking aloud. This was the true gift of the tribe, one of the fringe benefits they could never have anticipated when they signed up to come here, an unexpected blessing from the people she was supposedly here to help.

It had been especially difficult for her to learn to stop chattering. The old habits of talking at the kitchen table with her neighbors, her sisters, her daughter, the coffee pot always on. Well, it had taken some effort on her part to change. God knew what He was doing, however. As usual. Why was she always surprised by God? *The aggravation we could all save ourselves,* she thought, *if we would just listen to the leading of the Holy Spirit right away.* To remember that Jesus Himself found it necessary to leave the disciples and find a place for quiet. That He had prayed for guidance and direction and, yes, even courage in the garden of Gethsemane. How beautiful His struggle had been in Matthew 26.

> O my Father, if it is possible, let this
> cup pass from Me; nevertheless, not as I
> will, but as thou wilt.

What a picture of perfect obedience. Her own life fell far short of that ideal. Yet she strived for that kind of maturity, and the striving had given her a stronger marriage as well as a stronger faith.

The stillness of the jungle was unnerving her. She moved slowly, unsure of herself, unsettled. Evil was here. She could sense its presence—real and alive and breathing. She sensed powerful spiritual warfare, and a verse sprung to her lips.

> For we wrestle not against flesh and
> blood, but against principalities, against
> powers, against the rulers of the darkness
> of this world, against spiritual wickedness
> in high places. (Ephesians 6:12)

She moved out into the night. Jack was right behind her when they both suddenly stopped in their tracks. *Voices.* They could hear voices coming from the river. They looked at each other in confusion. What was going on? These raids always happened in the early morning or at night silently, swiftly with the rebels coming and striking and then taking off before a counterattack could be raised. Often they would only be hiding for a short time before the all clear when the women and young children would come slowly out of the forest and back into camp, picking the work back up and moving through another day.

She was drifting again. She struggled to focus as they made their way deeper into the jungle. She prayed for protection because she couldn't shake the sense of evil pervading the air. She prayed for the protection of the tribe. The people she was trying to reach for Jesus.

Help us, Lord, she thought to herself. *Keep our enemies far from us.*

Jack stilled her with a touch, and she felt her eyes tearing when she realized his hand was trembling. They stopped. She couldn't see very far in front of her, but suddenly, she knew that they were being watched. She swallowed convulsively. Her eyes were darting around looking for the threat. Jack was moving his head back and forth, peering intently into the dark. She could hear the fear in her own breathing. It was loud and ragged, like the breath was being ripped from her. She tried to be quiet, willed herself to be invisible. Fear like she had never known gripped her even as she repeated to herself.

> For God hath not given us a spirit
> of fear, but of power, and of love, and of
> a sound mind. (2 Timothy 1:7)

The scripture calmed her as it always did. Her heartbeat slowed down.

Movement—she sensed it before she saw it. The men seemed to drop from the air in front of her. Behind her. Jack grunted and staggered knocking into her. She opened her mouth in a horrified, "Oh," as his weight knocked her off balance. She stumbled forward and was suddenly looking into the cold eyes of a man who grinned wildly at her. She felt something warm on her skin, then a stinging pain, confusion as her body fell to the jungle floor not obeying her thought to move.

So fast, she thought. *So fast.*

11

CHAPTER *1*

. . . .

JEN REMEMBERED A LINE from a Greek writer.

In our sleep, pain which cannot forget
falls drop by drop upon the heart
Until in our own despair, against our will,
comes wisdom through the awful grace of God.
(Aeschylus)

It was supposed to be an adventure of a lifetime—a trip halfway around the world to minister the Gospel. Naively, it never crossed Jenny's mind that her parents would be anything but totally safe and secure. The Bible was full of people who had been killed or hurt for their faith. But *they* were heroes and martyrs. Jen never saw her parents in that light. Her mom and dad's deaths were sudden and horrible. They were murdered. It had shattered her boring and safe life into a million tiny fragments of phone calls, tears, nightmares, and funeral arrangements.

She even tried to repeat a Bible verse, but for once, she found no comfort in the words. *Death, where is thy sting? Grave, where is thy victory?* Pain filled her heart and mind. It felt to her like the grave had won, and it did sting. She knew that now was the time to be clinging to the cross she had so recently embraced, but she was overwhelmed with doubt.

The pastor had prayed for her, but she couldn't, wouldn't participate. She merely listened to him, his voice—an annoying buzzing in her head—and kept her mouth shut.

She never so much as took an aspirin when she had a headache, but after her parent's death, when Dr. Riordan had suggested some sleeping pills, she took them without hesitation. She wanted to sleep, not feel.

Exhaustion hung on her, weighing her down. It was a huge effort to get up and get dressed. Church members brought more food than she would ever eat. Everyone whispered and flashed worried glances. She spent a lot of time in her room, curled up in a fetal position, wishing she was just a kid again.

Her brother, Todd, seemed to be doing better. After her hysterical phone call, he and his wife, Caroline, were at the house by noon the following day. It was comforting to hear people moving around downstairs. She hadn't realized how much she missed having other people in the house. Todd was even helping with the funeral arrangements though certainly talking with the pastor was not his cup of tea.

"Why did You let this happen?" her heart cried out to God.

She sobbed into the purple satin pillow on her bed that she had ordered from a specialty store in California, completely ruining it. All she could do was continue her big heaping sobs that came from her gut and made her feel worse.

Todd came into her room and walked to the window. He cranked it open, letting the scent of pine needles penetrate the suffocating gloom. Shaking his head in sympathy, he moved to the bed and sat down next to her.

"You're all right, Jen," he said, patting her back. "It's okay."

She bolted upright in the bed angrily, knocking Todd's arm away. "It's not okay, Todd. It's never going to be okay again." She swiped furiously at the tears rolling down her face. She jumped out of the bed and began pacing, beating an angry path from the window to the bed. "How dare He?" she shouted. "How dare God do this to me? To us. To them! They were doing His work!"

Todd shrugged his shoulders and spoke, "I don't know what to say, Jen. I really don't. I'm not sure I think it's anyone's fault. They were just in a really dangerous part of the world."

"It's not fair, Todd," she said, sagging back down onto the bed. "It's just not fair."

The tears were silently running down her face again, and she made no move to wipe them. Her anger evaporated as suddenly as it had come. In its place was a coldness that began to take a deep hold in the recesses of her heart.

Her brother got up again and grabbed the box of tissues that were sitting on top of the dresser. He handed them to her, and she mechanically took one.

"I'm only twenty-two." She pushed her dirty brown hair out of her eyes and looked at him sadly. "Dad was supposed to walk me down the aisle when I got married. Mom was supposed to babysit my kids." A hiccup startled her, and she sank back down onto the pillows. She felt sicker than she ever had, believing in her heart of hearts this was God's fault.

Todd would never understand that. He didn't believe in God enough to blame Him. Todd patted her back and soothed her with his voice until she closed her eyes. She heard him tiptoe out of the room as she dropped off into an uneasy sleep.

After only several days, once the funeral was over, Todd and Caroline went back to their busy lives in Seattle. The next two weeks, Jenny had nightmares about masked men stabbing her to death. Some nights, she woke up screaming, soaked in sweat. Some nights, she stumbled to the bathroom and threw up whatever was in her stomach. The days felt even worse. Everything that used to be normal was all different now.

Nothing was the same anymore and even she knew that she was avoiding everyone and everything. It seemed like people had begun to realize this as she kept getting calls from old friends and people from church. She went to the coffee shop for work when she absolutely had to then came home and crashed in front of the television until she fell asleep on the couch. She had pulled on her jeans this morning and realized she was floating in them. She couldn't remember the last time she had eaten a good dinner. Normally, she would have been thrilled to be shedding pounds off her chubby frame, but now she simply couldn't bring herself to care at all. The days passed in a blur.

*****

Wednesday night, Bible study had been her regular routine before her parents were killed, but this time, she only came because she had committed to helping Shirley with this project months ago. Shirley was a good friend and a great teacher; her classes were the most popular in the entire church with the adults, and her lessons were so down to earth that Jen found herself paying close attention despite her efforts not to.

"So you see," Shirley said, "after all that Job went through, he never sinned and never blamed God. His belief was that God had given him everything and if God chose to could take it all back." Jen shifted uncomfortably in her seat. She tried hard to ignore the conviction she was starting to feel after listening to the story of Job.

Shirley continued softly, tucking a stray piece of blond hair behind her ear, "Hard to believe that someone could face those kinds of trials and maintain that kind of faith, isn't it? He lost his kids. He lost his money. His wife told him to curse God and die. His friends figured he must have sinned. How could he still believe that God was good and faithful?" She paused and looked searchingly at everyone. "Yet there it is for us to read and learn from." Her face grew serious. "Listen, folks, the Bible is the same yesterday, today, and forever. The kind of faith you see displayed here in Job can be your faith. It is within your grasp. Job grieved his losses. He wasn't superhuman, but he did the one thing that changed everything. When everything was at its very worst, Job looked to his Creator, and that made all the difference. When we have problems, we cry, moan, complain, seek counseling, talk to our friends, and ask our moms' advice."

Jen sucked in a quick breath of pain as Shirley paused; the other women in class were erupting into laughter.

"Never too old to talk to our moms, are we? But seek God? Last on the list. How can we feel better? By drawing God closer to us. What draws Him? Worship. *Draw close to God, and He will draw close to you.* Job kept pushing to get to God because he knew it was ultimately God that was in control. No matter what you are going through, the lesson to be learned from Job is that Job never turned *from* God but always turned *to* God. Got it? Okay, we're done." Shirley closed her notebook.

The room was still and quiet as everyone seemed to be reflecting on the lesson. Soon the people in the room began to slowly move forward for group prayer. Jenny stayed in her seat in the back, watching the people join hands in a circle. Her heart was heavy, and she remained in her seat even after the first prayers began. She looked down at the threadbare blue carpet that needed replacing and bit her lip desperately, trying to hold back tears.

As the prayers continued, she pushed herself up and out of her seat and quietly left.

CHAPTER 2

JENNY HOPPED UP AND down on one foot and then the other. "It's frr…freezing," she said, her teeth chattering as every cell in her body shivered. She hated coming home from work in the cold. How many winters had she spent in this frigid country? Oh yeah, twenty-two! How many more Ketchikan winters would she endure before she had the courage to migrate to a warmer climate?

She had dropped her coffee this morning when she was getting in the car, and the coffee that had spilled out had frozen into what looked like a melted blob of chocolate. Interesting, yes, but also annoying. *California.* What she wouldn't do to live in California? These ideas ran circles in her mind as she tried to open the iced-over mailbox.

To leave the family house was not something she could bring herself to do. It was the final link to her parents and the place where all her memories were stored. *And the cost of moving. And what would she do for a job?* She shook her head and pushed the thoughts from her mind.

A move was not in her immediate future. Bracing her foot against the post, she pulled with all her five-foot two-inch might and broke the frozen seal on the mailbox.

Hugging the envelopes close to her body, she began the trek up the front door of the house. The path was slippery, forcing her to slow down. Her foot found an icy patch, and her arms flailed as she nearly lost her balance. The mail slipped from her gloved fingers. *Oh, great. This is great,* she thought as she looked down at the mail.

Bending over was difficult in her parka and snow pants, but the envelope postmarked "Trinidad and Tobago" caught her eye. Warmth rushed over her as she recognized the handwriting of her friend Laura. A smile started in her heart then spread from her freezing toes to the top of her stocking capped head. Eagerly, she scooped up the mail from the ground and turned back to the house. Closing the front door with her foot, she threw the rest of the mail on the table and raced up the stairs. The serenity of her room was the perfect place to get the latest news from the mission field of Trinidad.

Layers of clothing fell to the floor as Jenny undressed. She let her work clothes lay in a heap where they dropped and pulled on her favorite sweatpants and her super comfortable, super roomy blue-and-white UCLA sweatshirt— the one Todd had brought her back from a business trip to California. It was so overused it was beginning to develop holes. She wiggled into a warm comfortable cocoon on her bed. Surrounding herself with two giant goose down pillows, she settled in to read.

Jenny and Laura had reconnected after Jenny's parents had died. They had known each other as children and had gone to high school together. Laura had moved right after graduation and then into the mission field. Jenny had never understood why it mattered enough for her to go across the world to Trinidad, and the two of them had lost contact.

In the first letter Jenny had received from her, Laura had written about having a dream from God and waking up feeling like she needed to reach out to her and to rekindle the friendship that had faded away. She also explained why she was sending a letter rather than finding her e-mail or on Facebook. She had spotty connections where she was, and while she couldn't always get computer access, someone was always going into the nearest town and could post a letter. Even the sympathy cards from people she was close to had not helped her feel any better after her parents died, but Jenny was consoled by Laura's letter. She had written back immediately, and the correspondence had continued from then on.

They talked about everything now, and with the letter still unopened in her hands, Jenny thought about the last letter she had sent to Laura. She had talked about her parents, about watching *Anne of Green Gables* for the hundredth time, about how Alaska was nothing like Green Gables, and about the difficulty she was having with being stuck and not connecting with people. She looked over at the pictures she had framed on her nightstand—a great shot of her parents at the annual Fourth of July picnic, Todd and Caroline's wedding photograph, and a picture of Laura standing in front of her church in Trinidad. Smiling at the picture of Laura, she slowly unfolded the pages of her letter, anxious to read the response from her last letter.

> *Dear Jenny,*
> *I'm sorry about feeling like you are stuck right now. You sound so discouraged. PLEASE DON'T BE! God does care for you. There is nothing going on that He can't see. I know it's tough, but I believe that He is there with you as you go on with your life. Even though you don't have someone going through life with you in this season, just think the right guy could be right around the corner. I know it is hard to wait, but*

you have had so much turmoil in your life already, perhaps a relationship is not what is best? I remember you saying even in high school that you wanted to move away from Alaska. I've been praying for you and will keep on praying that you will be in the right place for you. And I am praying that you would meet the right guy at the right time. But for now, be patient and wait on God. His love and care can really change things in our lives. I've seen for myself what happens when I open up to God. He is a good God, and He has good things in store for you. Not just in heaven but here too. I've been praying for you. Pray for me too!

Jenny paused. Hearing from Laura's perspective was refreshing. She seemed more spiritually mature than Jenny; it didn't seem like she felt like she was missing out on anything at all, even though she was so far away. She tried to think about God the way Laura did as someone who loved her, as someone who wanted to bless her.

The image of her parents dying brutally murdered in a jungle flashed through her mind. She sat still with the letter in her hand for some time. She had always heard that God was good, and even with her circumstances, she wanted to believe it.

The envelope and letter slowly slipped off her lap and onto the bed beside her. She missed the way her dad used to pat her on the head. She missed their Saturday breakfasts together at the coffee shop. She desperately missed her mom's hugs; those touches had made her *feel* loved. She missed her parents. She missed Todd, even though they never agreed on anything. She hated being alone every day in a big drafty house. She wanted to belong somewhere. She wanted to belong to someone.

Her mom and dad would have made wonderful grand-parents. Tears flooded Jenny's eyes, and she wiped them dry again, breathing heavily. Every time she was sure she was done grieving or at least the crying part of grieving, the tears would come at some unexpected memory.

She hated feeling melancholy, but she had learned from a grief counselor she had seen last year to just let the feelings in and ride the wave. So she did. Hunger finally drove her back downstairs, and she lost herself in cooking. The grief was easier to deal with and didn't last as long anymore. *Time does help*, she thought. *I guess it's not just a saying.*

CHAPTER *3*

. . . .

TODD SAT AT HIS desk and clicked on his inbox. He groaned audibly when he saw the mailbox was full again. Ever since he had run the piece about his parent's death, dozens of readers had responded. At first, he tried to answer each one personally, but he couldn't keep up this pace much longer, not in addition to all his regular work. Celia had offered to help. He hated to use the interns for his work, but now it was becoming almost a necessity.

The story had run on the cover of the *Seattle Times* Sunday edition. The piece had been difficult for him to write; it was a departure for him to add emotion to his writing, which was usually nothing but facts. Mitch, his editor, warned him to expect a lot of responses. It was the only personal piece he could ever remember writing.

As he read up on the political instability of the Philippines, he was amazed that even in the modern world, these atrocities could still be taking place. People were kidnapped and ransomed. People were burned alive, hacked to death with machetes. He was not the type of man who cried easily, but he found himself in the stall one day—after some research about machetes—dry-heaving into the toilet with tears streaming down his face. It was his mom, for God's sake.

How could a man do that? What kind of man could do that to a woman? The memory of visiting Jenny ran through his mind. Each night, when he was with her, she was having nightmares about it. The first time he heard Jen screaming bloody murder, he rushed into her room. She was sitting up in bed, sobbing, covered in sweat. He had never seen her like this before. Todd's stomach churned.

She was rocking back and forth and shaking her head and saying, "No, no, please," over and over.

Caroline had appeared wide eyed in the doorway a minute behind him as he sat holding his sister on the bed as they looked helplessly at each other, and he remembered thinking it would be a miracle to make it through this.

He was glad she had her religion and had reconnected with an old friend. He remembered Laura from when they were kids. She was always with his sister. He remembered her being pretty. Quiet but pretty. She seemed to have a good head on her shoulders. Old fashioned but nice. She had become a missionary like his parents. It gave Jen something to hold onto and help her. Whatever got her through was okay by him, although personally, he felt that religion was a crutch.

He moved down the emails, glancing at the subject line to see if anything needed taking care of immediately. He double-clicked on one from Mitch and checked the clock. Mitch wanted to see him as soon as he was available. He picked up the phone and dialed.

"Good morning. Mitch Harting's office." The pleasant voice of Mitch's unflappable secretary, Donna, never changed even on the days when Mitch was on a tyrannical power binge as the *Seattle Times* editor in chief.

"Hey, Donna. It's Todd. The boss wanted to see me?" He tapped his pencil next to the pad of paper by his phone anxiously.

"He sure does, Todd, and it must be important. I can see him pacing in his office. Are you coming up?"

Todd responded in the positive and stood up from his chair, setting the phone back down in the cradle. Todd knew that Donna had a soft spot for him. She always referred to him as their star reporter.

When he arrived, Donna smiled broadly at Todd and then pitched her voice low, said in a conspirator's tone, "He's all excited about something!" She looked around, checking to see if anyone was listening. "Must be big!" she finished in a loud stage whisper.

Todd laughed out loud. She was truly something. Playing into the drama, he leaned in and drawled, "Well, I'll just go see about that if it's alright with you."

Donna laughed delightedly at his flirting and waved him by her and into the newspaper's inner sanctum.

"Come in, come in, Todd. Sit down. Do you want some coffee?" Mitch was already pouring two cups from his stash in the corner. Todd took the cup from Mitch's hand and sunk into the worn couch against the wall by the door without an invitation. He had been through these kinds of bull sessions a million times with his boss. Mitch sank into his desk chair and for a moment stared out the window at the street below.

"So what's up, Mitch?" Todd asked, annoyed with Mitch's dramatics when he knew he had a thousand e-mails waiting for him downstairs.

Mitch turned back from the outside world to look at Todd. "Todd, when's the last time you were home?" he asked, frowning slightly.

The question took Todd completely by surprise. Startled, he spilled some of his coffee and frantically mopped at his pants while thinking, *Where had that come from?* Mitch rarely, if ever, asked him about his personal life other than the cursory "How's your wife, Caroline? How's your sister?" type of questions.

"I don't know. I guess it was just after my parents died to help Jenny get the house situation under control. Why?"

Mitch hesitated. "Look, Todd, I know how you feel about going back to Alaska—"

"It's not that I mind going, but I—"

"But here's the deal." Mitch cut off Todd's quick disagreement with a wave. "There's something big happening there with the oil industry, and I want you to go down there and start nosing around. I have a source that says some major changes are coming, and I want you on it. I'll give you a couple of weeks to pull something together for a special piece, something for another Sunday run. I want you there by the middle of next week. Donna can put together the details."

The way Mitch phrased it, Todd knew he was not being *asked* to go; he was being *told* to go. Normally, he loved the chance to delve into a new story. But he did not want to go to Alaska.

Todd couldn't put a finger on his own hesitation other than he didn't see the point in stirring up things that were better left alone—*feelings* that were better left alone.

Jenny was finally doing okay. The house was paid off thanks to his parent's insurance money so she could stay there if she wanted and wouldn't need his help.

This might be just the opportunity he needed to get some personal time to shake off his last story and delve into something completely different.

The myriad of things to do began to take shape in his mind. *He needed to get a hold of Caroline and tell her he was leaving. He needed to call his sister. Jenny at least would be thrilled. He needed to get a hold of his assistant, and he needed to touch base with the tech guys.*

"Okay, Mitch. I'll get a hold of my sister and tell her I'm coming and get the computer guys to tweak my computer. It's been giving me some problems with remote access."

Mitch herded him out of his office, probably hoping to cut him off before he could come up with an argument about sending someone else.

"Sounds good, Todd, whatever you need."

*****

Caroline was watching TV when he came in. One of those shows where the low-life's of America were paraded around on stage. They cursed and moaned about who was sleeping with who and who's the real daddy of some girl's baby—all in front of a television audience yelling out ugly things to add to the carnival atmosphere. He hated these talk shows, but Caroline loved them. She was glued to the television and laughed at the screen, barely looking up when he came in. He crossed in front of her to yank the chain on the fan to high coughing and waving his hand back and forth in the air. She was smoking—another thing he couldn't stand.

"Todd, get out of the way. I can't see."

"Well, I can't breathe with that smoke! What happened to our agreement? You're supposed to smoke outside. Why do we have discussions about this stuff if you aren't going to bother to actually follow through?" His look must have conveyed real annoyance because she rolled her eyes but put out the cigarette.

"Oh, relax, Todd. It's just one cigarette. For your information, I was going to go outside, but I didn't want to miss this." Her eyes were drawn back to the screen, and she laughed again as the two girls on stage started going at each other and had to be physically restrained by men who looked like bouncers.

Todd left the room, heading for the kitchen. "Hey, did you eat yet?" They never waited for each other to eat because they both had such crazy schedules; they never knew when they would be able to sit down together.

A commercial was playing as Caroline wandered into the kitchen and plopped down on a chair.

"I had some pasta. There is some left in the fridge."

He opened the fridge and pulled out the pasta, along with parmesan cheese.

"Do we have any bread?" He was looking helplessly at the counter.

Caroline rolled her eyes. She did that a lot with him. Popping up out of the chair, she reached across him to the toaster, knocking him out of the way.

"Hey," he protested weakly.

She pulled the bread out from behind the toaster where it had fallen.

Note to self, he thought, *remember to look before asking.*

He undid the twist tie and put a piece on his plate. He sat down at the table, and after adding some mustard, he ate his meal cold. He made the mistake of looking at Caroline's disgusted face.

"What?" he said with his mouth full.

She just shook her head and got up from the table. As she walked out of the room, she tossed back over her shoulder, "Honestly, Todd, you can be so gross."

"What's gross?" he called to her retreating back. Wiping mustard from his face, he shrugged, muttering under his breath, "Whatever."

Todd found her in the bedroom later, lying down. He sank down on the bed and started untying his gym shoes.

"Caroline, I have to talk to you."

"Yeah, what about?" she asked offhandedly.

"Mitch wants me to go to Alaska to work on a story."

Caroline sat up suddenly interested. "What's going on in Alaska?" she wondered, puzzled. "I haven't heard anything on the news."

"It's something to do with the oil there. Mitch thinks it could be another Sunday special." He couldn't keep a note of pride out of his voice.

"That's awesome, Todd," she said with real enthusiasm. "That raise we've been talking about is becoming a real possibility. Mitch can't say no if you get another response to your work like the one about your mom! They must have made a million bucks on that run. Everyone at my work read it, even the people who usually read the *Star*."

Todd beamed at her praise. Running a hand through his brown curly hair, he agreed with her. "I figure I might be gone a while though," he said cautiously. "From what I've heard, things can get a little tricky with the oil guys. No one likes to speak in front of anyone else. You know, real cloak and dagger stuff."

"That's fine by me, hon. Stay down there as long as you need too. We could really use that raise."

Todd detected an odd tone in her voice but was too excited to dwell on it and honestly, too tired to care. He was wiped. "I'll get that raise for you," Todd said, sinking onto the bed next to her. "Guaranteed."

CHAPTER 4

TODD SET UP SHOP in the house with Jenny's blessing. He set up his computer, printer, and scanner in the living room, making the corner of the living room a makeshift office. He spent the first week interviewing anyone who was willing to talk to him. Alyeska Pipeline Service Company had been incorporated in 1970. His dad had buddies that had worked there, and he knew he could still find friends of the family to speak with him.

The Trans-Alaska Pipeline System was very important and very entrenched in the minds of Alaskans. He also wanted to speak with the new kids on the block—BluePoint Energy. They were privately held, and the community, notoriously suspicious of outsiders, gave them a wide berth as they tried to acquire land and explore.

He attended the town hall meeting that had been set up to give a platform so that all sides could speak.

Oil was a big business in Alaska; it seemed that everyone had an opinion, and everyone wanted him to write about it. He did not lack for material.

Todd sat in the back of the meeting, admiring the poise of the representatives of the big three: BP, ExxonMobil, and ConocoPhillips. The situation had not changed much in the decade since Mr. Marks, the director of the state Division of Oil and Gas, had made an argument for the benefits of competition. He noticed the suits in the first row looking uneasily at the young guy on the end of the aisle wearing jeans and a flannel, the BluePoint guy, who had shaken quite a few hands when he walked in. He smiled and took a seat in the front just slightly apart from the other oil guys.

Todd made a note on his pad to make an appointment with him. He did a quick Google search and learned that the guy in the front row was Dallas Gorski, VP of strategy and exploration, thirty-five, a graduate of Harvard business. Todd looked glanced at the jean-wearing executive and wondered what he was playing at. He was a Harvard grad and was coming off the last five years overseeing Mexico and Venezuela per his bio. Todd wondered how he was going to get through a winter in Ketchikan after all that time in a warm climate.

"Good luck, buddy," Todd mumbled under his breath.

The mayor stepped up to the podium and called the meeting to order. Todd noticed that Dallas Gorski leaned in interested while the big three suits never looked up from their respective phones. As they collectively tapped out messages and scrolled through their feeds, Todd chuckled to himself. They were either very bored or very busy.

"We are going to limit remarks to five minutes, so we're not here until midnight," the mayor stated, looking out at the crowd. "Please keep your question pertinent. We are not here to vent."

Some grumbling emerged from those not seated in the first row. Todd heard an, "*Easy for you to say*," from somewhere behind and to the right of him. The mayor heard it too from the look of exasperation on his face.

"Roy," the mayor remarked, "perhaps you would like to start?"

A tall and weathered-looking guy with short-cropped gray hair stood up, removing his cap and squared his shoulders. "Well, mayor, we've been down this road before. These guys," he said, gesturing to the front row "want more access, but they don't want to pay more. This is our home, our land, and we want the drilling, but we need to be paid for it."

A smattering of applause broke as he sat back down in his aluminum chair.

The BP guy raised his hand. "If I may, Mayor?"

The mayor nodded his okay.

"Hi, I'm Ed for the few new faces. I represent BP. Roy, I believe we have always been fair in our dealings with you and everyone here in Ketchikan. We have spent years here working alongside all of you. If the government opens the new land for development, we just want the same opportunities you have already given us in the past to make a good deal—a solid deal with all of you." He sat back down, glancing around at his audience with the appearance of absolute ease.

Todd was taking notes and watching the faces to gauge reactions. Quite a few of the men around Roy were nodding in the affirmative.

Another hand went up, and the mayor pointed at a young guy with longish hair midway back in the center. "Why are we acting like this is a done deal? Even if they say yes to the drilling, why would we continue with something so devastating to the environment? I don't think it should be allowed at all."

There were some groans from the audience. Todd heard someone near him mutter, "Hippy," just loud enough for the guy to hear.

The guy's ears burned red as he defiantly looked around. "It's a valid opinion," he said strongly and seemingly satisfied sat back down.

The dialogue went back and forth like that for another hour. The oil executives were starting to fidget in their chairs.

Todd glanced at this phone. It was 10:00 p.m. He sighed, wondering if he could sneak out soon. He would have already left except he wanted to introduce himself to Dallas Gorski. At that moment, the mayor stepped up.

"All right. We've made a lot of progress tonight. Let's continue the dialogue with one another, and we will pick this back up next month at the town meeting."

Todd started to gather his things and stepping into the aisle made his way to the front. He would introduce himself to Gorski and see if it led anywhere.

*****

He posted articles by e-mail to Mitch who edited and sent them back for adjustments. He tried to find every angle and kept odd hours. He spoke to Dallas who turned out to be a down to earth Ivy Leaguer about the challenges of a massive capital investment into an area with such price and demand volatility and got a very thoughtful front-page piece from his response. Some of the players involved wouldn't talk to him in public but insisted he meet them in secret late at night. These were the guys who were talking about government regulations, becoming such a burden that companies were routinely skirting rules and the risk/rewards. It was equal parts fascinating and disturbing, and he had never worked so hard on a project. He was now an expert on the inner working of the oil business but exhausted from the effort. It felt like he had been away from home for years instead of months, and he couldn't wait to see Caroline again. He just had a few weeks left, and the paper would move off this subject—another news cycle had come to an end.

Todd turned the car off and rested his head on the steering wheel for a moment. It was late. Yawning, he looked blankly at the clock and groaned at the number displayed. It was 2:00 a.m. *Ugh.* He got out of the car, remembering not to slam the car door and walked wearily to the front door. He was coming from one of those secret meetings with one of the big shot oil guys at BP. It had been a pointless meeting. The guy didn't have anything to share of substance; he just wanted to make sure his company was being represented in a favorable light.

Todd quietly headed upstairs to crash. He tiptoed down the hall but stopped when he heard voices coming from Jenny's room. He paused and cocked his head. He moved closer, stopping at Jenny's door to listen. It was kind of late for her to be watching television, he thought, looking at his watch and wincing as the digital readout glowed 2:10 a.m. Was she having another nightmare? He stood at the door and listened.

"Lord, You know how he is. He's always been hesitant about you. He thought it was weird when Mom and Dad got saved, and he was really weirded out when I got saved. It must be so hard for him, Lord. Not knowing You, he must think I'm crazy. He's working so hard, Lord, but for what? He doesn't know You, and I'm so scared, Father—so scared something will happen to him, and I want him to know You so much! To be comforted by You. To be guided by You. Please send Your spirit to Todd and stir him, Father."

He took a step back suddenly when he realized she was praying. *This late?* He suddenly felt guilty for standing there and listening, but he also couldn't seem to tear himself away. She was talking to God like He was a close friend.

As he took in the words, he heard Jenny praying for his protection, his marriage, and his soul. *His soul?* He never gave any thought to his soul—not as a reality anyway, more of a concept. Something everyone had.

Stepping back from the door, he rubbed his eyes and couldn't keep another yawn at bay. He took one last look at Jen's door and then turned to head down the hall to his own room. He dropped down on the bed still in his clothes, kicking off his shoes and laying back, closed his eyes. Drifting off to sleep, his last thought was, *Wow, my sister loves me enough to pray for me at two o'clock in the morning.*

That Sunday, when Jenny asked him to go to church, which she had done every single Sunday since the first week, it finally registered how important it must be to her. *I can be kinda pigheaded.*

"Todd, yo—where did you go?" Jenny waved a hand in front of his face. "Do you think you might want to go this morning?"

Todd sipped his coffee and looked across the table at his sister. "You know what?" Todd said. "Yeah. I'll come. You spend so much time there. I should check it out." Todd watched her trying to cover her surprise and act cool but was entertained by how big her eyes got. She had obviously been expecting his usual excuses.

"Great! *Umm.* Okay. I leave at 10:00. Can you be ready?"

"Yup. I'll get dressed." Todd hit the stairs chuckling to himself. He could tell she was thrilled. *And that, my friends, is how you do the big brother thing, right?*

The service, however, was not what he expected, and he wondered right away what he had gotten himself into. Until his parents had changed religions, they had considered themselves Catholic. He was never sure what that meant, except that once in a while, usually on holidays, they went as a family to church and participated in whatever—stand, sit, kneel, repeat. Everything ordered and neat. Jenny's church was very, very different.

"Hi, welcome! Oh my god, are you Jenny's brother? We are so glad you're here!" The bubbly blond usher was enveloping him in a hug before he could get a word out.

"Ugh, yeah, hi." Jenny pulled him along laughing at his discomfort.

"Don't be a brat," he whispered out of the side of his mouth.

Jenny laughed out loud as she smiled at him and took a seat.

Todd looked around and marveled at the crowd. Ketchikan was a small place, and it felt like the whole town might be in this building today. He waved at some old-school friends who immediately walked over to shake hands and welcome him.

"Todd, so glad to see you. I heard you were in town. So good to see you." He heard the same welcome ten times before the people on stage started playing their instruments.

"Welcome, friends. Let's stand to our feet and worship the Lord!"

Everyone stood to their feet. *I can't picture my parents here. It's so different than Our Lady of Fatima.*

Everyone seemed excited to be there on a regular Sunday. He would check the calendar when he got home, but he was almost sure this was not a holiday. A ton of people had Bibles—some of considerable sizes, which he felt was a bit showy.

The pastor took the mike and looked out at the crowd. "Welcome home! We are excited you chose to worship with us today. Is anyone here for the first time?"

Todd tried to slouch in his seat to go unnoticed, but Jenny was putting his arm up for him. He gave her an embarrassed glare. A few other people had their hands up, thank God, or he would have died.

"We here at Abundant Life not only love the Lord, but we also love people. So why don't you turn around and greet four or five people? For all of you introverts, we put one minute on the screens. You only have to socialize for one minute, and you're done. For all of you extroverts, you only have one minute, so try to contain yourselves!"

Everyone laughed as people erupted from their seats to meet and greet each other and then sat back down after the time ran out.

Todd sat back and settled in to listen to the priest. *Pastor, not priest. I must remember that.*

It seemed like everyone under thirty had their phones out. *Typical millennials.* He was sneaking looks at the kid in front of him, curious as to what he was looking at, and realized he wasn't on Facebook; he was reading the Bible, *huh*! Even if he had his own Bible to tote in here, he would never have been able to find the books that the pastor was referencing. He had not spent much time reading the Bible. Some of the names were vaguely familiar, but others he knew he had never heard before. *Who is Esther? Why had he never heard of Esther?*

Todd glanced surreptitiously down at his phone. One o'clock! He realized that they had been in church for two hours! He was tired and hungry and resolved that one visit was enough. He hoped Jenny would be satisfied with the effort he had made today.

"Please stand for dismissal."

Todd breathed a quick sigh of relief as he stood to his feet.

"Lord, thank You for who You are. You are mighty and a very present help in trouble. I pray for Your blessing and protection on Your people as they live out their Christlike walks this week and that You would extend traveling mercies to all that leave here today. We ask it in the name of Jesus."

"Amen."

As they got into the car to head home, Jenny turned to him expectantly. "Well, what did you think?"

He hated to hurt her feelings, so he didn't want to say too much. He shrugged noncommittally and said, "It was okay."

She looked crushed.

He groaned inside. *Great. Just great*, he thought. *Here I am trying to do the right thing, and does anyone appreciate it?*

He tried again. "It was kinda long, Jenny," he said as if that explained everything.

Now she was surprised.

He could see her gathering her thoughts.

"That's fair, I guess. Sometimes it can seem long. But you know what, Todd? We spend as much time at a movie or a football game and don't give it a second thought." She ended with a quiet "God sure does get shortchanged sometimes."

Feeling defensive, he let the subject drop. He felt so guilty about the whole thing though he went with her the following Sunday too. He told himself to relax, *Enjoy it. Pretend you're at a football game.* He looked for angles for a story so he wouldn't be wasting his time, and he kept finding reasons to keep going back.

*****

Todd poked his head into the kitchen where Jen was making a sandwich. "Jen, do you have an extra Bible I could use?"

The knife Jen was using to spread mayo on her sandwich skidded off the counter and hit the floor. "Wait, what?" Jen looked at him askance.

"I want to look up the story pastor referenced on Sunday."

"Yeah, sure. Use mine. It's sitting on the table in the living room."

"Thanks." Todd took off before more conversation could ensue. He didn't want to talk about what he was feeling yet. He just knew that something was changing.

*****

"Todd, great to see you're becoming a regular!" The pastor winked at him.

"Glad to be here, Pastor," Todd said and suddenly realized he meant it. *What is happening?* Before he knew it, he was looking forward to Sundays and even more unbelievable he had started to hear what the pastor was saying.

"So Abraham believed in God's promises. When God said go, he went because he knew he had an inheritance just like we do. Turn to Hebrews 11:8."

Todd listened attentively. He was feeling uncertain and starting to suspect he may be missing something important in his life. He was determined to investigate. To get to the bottom of the story. His story. He would approach this Christianity thing like he did everything. He would run it down. Feeling better about having a plan, he relaxed a little and waited for service to end.

*****

He practically started to cry when Jen came home the next day with a new Bible for him. She had written on the dedication page,

To my brother, Todd,
as you begin your journey.

Love, Jen

He sat with the Bible in his hand in the old lazy boy chair, and his eyes welled with tears. He hadn't cried like this when he lost his parents, but suddenly, his heart was breaking.

Jenny happened upon him as he sat reading. He had been reading for hours and was wiping tears from his eyes on his sleeve. He saw her out of the corner of his eye as she discreetly backed out of the room, pretending she hadn't seen anything.

He devoured his Bible. He couldn't explain it, but the verses seemed to have been written just for him.

He spent a week thinking about how to explain what was happening and then called home and tried to talk to Caroline about it. She laughed uproariously over the phone at him and gasped out, "Todd, come home. You are seriously losing it!"

Todd put the phone back in his pocket and frowned. *Geez, she doesn't need to be mean about it. I'm serious about this.*

Jenny sat down at the kitchen table across from him having walked in on the conversation and smiled. "Don't be upset with her. She doesn't mean anything by it. Faith is personal. It has to happen for people in their own timing, Todd. Think about how you reacted when Mom and Dad got saved? Then me? We tried to talk to you about our faith, and you thought we were crazy."

"Actually, I thought you guys were in some kind of cult. It was just such a big change. You guys wouldn't stop talking about Jesus. It was weird. I didn't get it."

Jenny quirked an eyebrow at him. "See? Just saying. Now you're doing it to Caroline, and she thinks you're crazy. So you are in a perfect situation to allow her some grace while you figure out what God means to you. Accepting Jesus will change your life, Todd. But it's worth it."

She had a point. He did remember thinking they had all gone crazy. He had been downright hostile toward their *religion* when his parents had gotten killed. Maybe Caroline would get it if he could get her to go to church when he got home.

He was winding up his story quickly. He had spoken with Mitch early that week, and they agreed that the oil story had been covered about as extensively as it could be. He figured on wrapping it up within the next week, and Mitch was ready to have him back in Seattle.

CHAPTER 5

· ·

TODD TURNED OFF ON seventh and parked at the trailhead of Rainbird Trail. He needed an easy hike to quiet his mind and help him to think. This whole church thing was weighing on him heavily. He couldn't put a finger on the feelings he was having except to say they felt burdensome. He wanted to take some time and really turn it over in his head and figured a short hike would be just the thing.

Sighing heavily, he shut off the car and got out. Leaning against the door, he looked out at the mountains. It was overcast, and the mountains looked blue against the gray sky. Taking a deep breath, he filled his lungs with air that was tinged with the smell of the nearby water and hoisted his day pack over his shoulder. Shoving his keys in his pocket, he headed left to the trail. He paused for a moment in front of the sign.

Welcome to the Rainbird Trail!

The University of Alaska Southeast Ketchikan welcomes you to the trailhead of the Rainbird Trail.

Made possible through the generous contributions of organizations and individuals in Southeast Alaska. The trail is approximately 1.3 miles long and takes you into the lush undergrowth of the Tongass National Forest. The top of the trail overlooks the city of Ketchikan the Tongass narrows and beyond. The trail is steep and rocky in spots and was built to minimize the overall impact to the environment. Parts of the trail require sure footing and may not be suitable for all the fitness levels.

Be safe and enjoy the view.

Todd smiled at the familiar sign. He had always loved the picture of the rainbird.

The logo was everywhere in Ketchikan—the mythical green-and-orange rainbird that is said to inhabit the local rain forest. The trail was easy other than being a little steep in the beginning. It was a relaxing hike that led to an overlook of the town and the port where the cruise ships came in.

When he and Jenny were younger, they hiked here frequently, and he planned on bringing his kids here too someday. Filled with huge trees, ferns, and berry bushes, the gravel surface quickly gave way to wooden steps.

Todd looked up as a float plane came into land and then shaking himself out of his reverie continued onto the trail.

Ten minutes later, he was huffing and puffing up the embankment. *He had been gone for years, and maybe it was harder and steeper than he remembered. He also wasn't twenty anymore.* Taking a breather, he leaned against the log rail and looked out at the water. *What am I doing?* He didn't move, just gazed out at the water allowing his cluttered mind to quiet itself.

The water was still as glass, and it was quiet in the port the next influx of tourists from the cruise ships not due until

Saturday. He missed this place. The pace was so different from Seattle—the quiet so easy to find. He felt like everything was about to shift for him, but he couldn't put a name to it. He just knew that he felt different.

His mom and dad had tried so hard to tell him about Jesus, but he wouldn't listen. How many arguments had he started? How many times had he cut them off when they broached the subject? Todd winced when he recalled one of the last times he had spoken to his parents. They were on a mandatory break and resting before resupplying in the largest town outside of their village.

His mom had been able to make a phone call from the charity headquarters, and he had rushed her off the phone when she started talking about God's goodness. Regret was a bitter pill. He looked up at the sky and spoke to the God, who had previously been a mystery to him and said simply, "I'm sorry."

Stifling a sob, he bent over at the waist, trying to control his emotions, and wept, "I'm so sorry. I need to know if You're real. I need to know You hear me. If You're real, please help me to find You."

*****

That final Sunday before he left Alaska, Todd responded with an upraised hand to the call of salvation. He spoke the confession of faith with everything that was in his heart. He surrendered his life and his future to Jesus. Publicly acknowledging the changes he knew had started in him weeks before, months before. He was thrilled and scared and, for the first time in his life, filled with hope.

*****

The airport wasn't crowded. Jenny pulled her VW convertible in the parking lot and shut off the car. She looked over at Todd, who was staring off to the east at the mountains.

"You ready?" she asked.

Todd glanced at her with a small smile. "Ready," he said.

Grunting, he opened the door and went around to the back of the car. Struggling to pull his bag out the small trunk, he complained out loud, "Jen, you need a bigger car. This is ridiculous. How do you even drive this thing in the winter?"

Jen smiled.

He had been making fun of her car since the day she bought it. He absolutely refused to be in it when she had the top down.

"Shut up, Todd," she said, knowing the bickering was delaying the inevitable goodbye. She was totally on board with delaying the inevitable. For the first time since they were kids, she could feel a sense of connection with him. She did not want to let him go.

They walked into the municipal airport entry, and Todd went up to the counter to check in. Jen looked around at the waiting area. Small and stuck in the 70s, the place was filled with plastic bucket seats and carpet, some weird combination of beige, blue, and orange. The latest improvement was a cell phone charging station they had installed in the corner of the room. Presently, that corner was filled with backpackers sprawled out on the floor, all charging their phones.

Jen watched a guy, maybe eighteen or nineteen, as he dumped his pack unceremoniously on the carpet. *What the heck was he looking for?* The boy sported a big grin as he pulled out a box of crackers and offered them to the group. Jen smiled at his simple pleasure. He then began to methodically roll his clothes into tight tubes and stuff them back in his pack. She was so engrossed she yelped when Todd touched her shoulder.

"C'mon, nut," Todd said mischievously. "I'm ready to go."

Jen's eyes suddenly filled with tears, and she fought them off with the tried and true trick of opening her eyes super wide and staring at the ceiling. As the tears started leaking down her face anyway, she thought about how stupid that was. *Who came up with that trick anyway? It. Did. Not. Work.*

Todd engulfed her in a hug. "I'll be back, Jen. It won't be as long the next time. I promise. I have a lot to talk to Caroline about, and to tell you the truth, I'm really nervous about it."

Jen, biting her lip anxiously, said, "It is going to be weird for her. Just think about how you used to feel about God, not to mention how I felt about God after Mom and Dad died. It's not easy to submit your life to God. Not if you've been a Christian for ten years or ten minutes."

"I *am* thinking about that," he replied with a shrug. "That's what has me worried." He grimaced.

"Okay," Jen said, "let's start this off right."

Todd looked at her puzzled.

"We can pray before you go," Jenny explained.

Todd looked surprised but suddenly eager too. "Right now?"

Jen nodded affirmatively.

"That's a great idea!" Todd agreed. "Umm, can you do it?"

Jen smiled even through her tears. She glanced around; the backpackers looked up for a moment before going back to their conversations.

"Let's sit down." Jenny led Tod over to some empty seats. Without waiting for him to close his eyes, she took his hands in hers and began her prayer, "Father God…"

CHAPTER *6*

. . . .

CAROLINE DID NOT MEET him at the airport. She never did even if she was home. He took too many trips, she complained, for her to be running to the airport every five minutes. Besides, she would always add, "You know, how the traffic is. Waste of time and gas when it's just as easy for you to Uber home on the paper's dollar." What could he say to that?

He walked into the apartment and set his bag down by the door. The television was off, and there was no sign of Caroline. He laid his jacket on a chair and went into the kitchen to rummage around for something to eat. It was only four so he thought he might wait to eat and see if Caroline wanted to go out to dinner when she got home. He found a bag of chips to snack on and went into the front room. He sat in his recliner, popped the lever, and let out a satisfied grunt as his feet were elevated. *Ah, now that's better*, he thought to himself. He flipped on the news and munched on the chips biding his time. An hour later, he heard keys in the door and waited for Caroline to come in before he called out to her, "Hey, there, beautiful!"

She came into the room, smiling and teasing him back, "Hey, handsome, you shouldn't be here, you know, my husband is due back from a trip any minute." She walked over and sat down on his lap, wrapping her arms around him and squeezed.

"Hey," he yelped, "watch the chips!" He saved them from getting crushed as laughing; she kissed him square on the mouth.

A minute later, they came up for air and smiled into each other's eyes.

"I missed you," they both said simultaneously then cracked up.

Caroline punched him lightly on the arm. "Jinx, you owe me a Coke."

"I'll do you better than that. How about I take my favorite girl out for dinner?"

Caroline jumped up. "Great! Let me change. I'm starving! How about that Italian place on Fifth Avenue... Tulio's?"

She didn't really expect him to answer obviously as she had already left the room. She knew he didn't care where they ate, and Tulio's did have great food. They had an appetizer: potato gnocchi with sage butter and cheese that was out of this world. *Yup*, he thought, *that sounds perfect*. It was a good place to have a talk too. Cozy.

*****

Big mistake, he thought belatedly. *I only mentioned that I wanted to go to church*. What was he thinking! Not only was she not interested, she was furious! She had practically knocked over her chair on her way out of Tulio's leaving him to get the check and hurry out of there. *Good thing I waited until I was done eating*, he thought morosely.

"What? Now you're a new person? You think you're better than everyone?"

The more he tried to inject, the angrier she got. He pleaded with her to let him explain, but she didn't want to hear any of it. That's when she had made her dramatic exit.

He didn't think the three glasses of wine she had at dinner helped his cause either. She was primed for a fight.

She was waiting by the car, tapping her foot impatiently when he walked to her side to unlock the door. She wouldn't make eye contact and maintained a frosty silence all the way home.

Upon entering the house, she had slammed the door in his face and retreated to the couch where she turned on the television with the volume up to an uncomfortable level.

"That's just to aggravate me," he muttered as he unlocked the door and let himself in. He promptly retreated to his office to assess his wounds. He turned on his computer and e-mailed Jenny who had finally broken down and gotten a new laptop to better keep in touch with him. He ended his latest spiritual update with a plea to Jenny, "Please keep praying! I don't know what to do."

He sat back and looked at the screen punched send and raked his hand through his hair; he decided to give the talk one more try. He walked into the front room and sat in the chair furthest from the couch. Who knew what she would throw at him when she was in one of her moods! He was brave, not stupid.

She gave him a withering look that almost caused him to flee the room. Maybe he wasn't as brave as he thought.

"Look, Caroline, I don't know what you're thinking—"

He tried to gather his thoughts, but she interrupted right away, "*Now* you're worried about what I'm thinking?" She spat out. "You should have been wondering *that* before you made some *life-altering* decision." She threw out the words he had used at the dinner table to describe how he was feeling.

They didn't sound right when she said them. He was sure he had not used that condescending tone.

He tried again, speaking slowly and carefully, "Car, it's a decision I made, yes, but I had every intention of talking with you about it. I want to share it with you, but my faith is my faith. I had to make the decision for myself just like you will." He kept going, speeding up, hoping that he could get it all in before she wouldn't listen anymore. "All I'm saying is this wonderful thing has happened to me, and I want to share it with you."

She was quiet for a minute. Then she looked at him. Her lips were compressed into a thin line. He had never seen her look so cold.

"Todd, listen to me and listen to me closely. I like my life. I like *our* life. Just. Like. It. Is." The words were punctuated with venom. "I don't want to change. I don't need some goofy religion, which, by the way, were your words for it not so long ago. You sure had plenty to say about it when your parents did the same thing to you. Let me repeat: I don't need some religion in my life. My life is fine. Our life is fine. If you think I am going to have a baby with some Holy Roller, you are sadly mistaken." She looked at him coldly.

He blinked. "Baby?"

She got up from the couch before he could put a sentence together; took her coat, keys, purse; and left, slamming the door for the second time that night.

Baby? Before he could think of something and yell, "Wait!" she was long gone.

Three days later, Todd was on the couch. He had called in sick to work two days in a row, and the lie only momentarily gave him pause. He was heartsick. He figured that had to count for something. He was beside himself with worry. Caroline had not been back to the house since the fight. He couldn't eat, couldn't sleep. He had called everyone he knew, trying to figure out where she had gone.

She had finally called from her mother's house that morning after calling work and finding out he wasn't there. He begged her to come back. He swore he would do anything to make their marriage work. He asked her hesitantly about the baby. She had started to cry, and all he could do was whisper into the phone, "Aw, sweetie, don't cry. C'mon, Caroline, it's okay. I'm thrilled about the baby."

She didn't want to hear anything about being saved or about church. When he tried to bring it up, she got hysterical. He decided to back off. He wouldn't bring it up again.

She agreed to come home, but it never did seem to work after that. She was sick during the pregnancy and blamed him. She continued to smoke and drink, which outraged him, and they continued to have huge blowups. The stress was starting to get to him, and despite the help and counsel of the pastor at his local church, his new walk with God was suffering.

Every time he left on Sunday morning to go to church, Caroline either pretended to be sleeping or just said no thanks. He didn't like her anymore, and the feeling was mutual. He knew that wasn't biblical, so he kept fasting and praying about it and holding on.

The New Year arrived along with the baby. Tyler Milner, 6 lbs, 6 oz, and 21 inches long with a head full of dark hair. Todd was glad he had finished up the nursery the week before.

Caroline had left everything to him. She had no interest in doing anything that had to do with the baby. He had picked out the crib and the dresser; he had decided on the colors.

Thank God for his sister, he thought.

He had started making more calls home, looking for advice and prayer. Jenny had encouraged him with everything. Toward the end, all Caroline did was to sit and watch television. The trash shows he hadn't liked before, and now that he was a Christian, it embarrassed and upset him. She could care less about his discomfort. She laughed at him. Her constant mocking always ended in her calling him a holy roller. He had counted on the baby bringing them closer, but it wasn't happening.

He came in from work every day and went straight to the bassinet. He couldn't get enough of that baby smell, the perfect fingers, and toes.

And then one day, he came home to his neighbor, watching the baby. Caroline was gone. She had taken off, leaving him and the baby behind. She left him a note that talked about how they were moving in different directions. How he just didn't *get her* anymore? He guessed he should be glad she had left the baby with a sitter. She has shown so little interest in him that it would not have surprised him if she had left him alone.

The devastation was overwhelming. He had sobbed into his hands at the kitchen table, not knowing what to do next. It wasn't so much missing Caroline as the feeling of failure—the sense that he should have been able to work this out. That it was his responsibility as the man of the household, as the man of God to keep it all together. He went over and over what he should have done differently, what he should have said differently. He should have prayed more, tried harder, gone slower, faster.

The recriminations overloaded him. He went to the bassinet and picked up the sleeping baby. He snuggled him in his arms, his chin touching the baby's head.

"What are we gonna do, buddy?" he whispered softly. "What are we gonna do?"

Todd stayed home the next day to watch the baby. He had called Jenny who was flying in that evening to help him figure something out. The first couple of weeks, they worked on a plan. He had never been so grateful for his sister. They went over all the different scenarios, and after a lot of prayer and a few calls back home, they finally came up with a workable solution.

Caroline had not called, and calls to her mother's house had not been returned. He expected that a lawyer would be contacting him at some point and left a forwarding phone and address on his mother-in-law's machine. Todd had explained the situation to Mitch and told him he was leaving the paper. Mitch, of course, had offered him anything he wanted to stay, but Todd felt that the Lord was leading him in a different direction.

He was going back to Alaska with Jenny. The local newspaper needed an editor, and they were thrilled Todd would even consider joining them. Some people might consider that a step-down, but Todd was learning that people measured success in different ways than God. He was going to be obedient to God and do the best he could to follow what he felt was God's leading.

CHAPTER 7

"HEY, JENNY, WAIT UP!" Steve yelled from across the street.

Jenny stopped with her hand on the door of Maggie Murphy's Mochas, the most popular coffee shop south of Juneau. Jenny loved working here. It was flexible hours, so she could be home with Tyler, and Maggie was easy about changes in scheduling—an absolute must with an active toddler at home.

She waited at the door for Steve to catch up. He headed across the street, dodging some guys in a jeep that were towing snowmobiles. Steve had moved here from Juneau after college to work as a ranger at the park. He had been a welcome addition to their small town. He quickly made friends with everyone, and every single girl that Jenny knew was trying to outdo the other to get his attention. He never even seemed to notice: treated all the girls the same and dated infrequently. She knew because she was not immune to him herself. Steve was drop dead gorgeous. The television star kind of handsome—tall, broad, dark with big blue eyes. Man, just looking at him made you want to straighten up or go home and change or something.

She smoothed her hair back and wished she had taken the time to put lipstick on. She was lazy about that in the winter. The lack of light just about did her in. Jenny checked her thoughts and issued a rueful smile at herself. God, better do something quick with her love life. She was starting to act and think like a hormone-driven teenager.

"Hey, Steve," Jenny smiled her most winning smile.

"Hey, Jenny," Steve smiled back just as broadly. He reached in front of her and pushed open the door to Maggie's for her.

"Do you have time to sit for a minute and talk, or do you have to start right away?"

Jenny looked at the nearly empty room. The only people in this morning were Dawn, who was wiping down the espresso machine and waved at them enthusiastically, and a couple of fishermen in a corner booth that looked like they had already put in a full day and were trying to warm up.

The coffeehouse was always slow in the winter after the tourists left for the season. Only the locals came in along with a few die-hard camping enthusiasts. Jenny found the summer loads more exciting. They were always meeting people from the cruises and stuff that were from all over the world—London, Paris, Australia, California. All of them sounded so different from Ketchikan.

She had been set on leaving since she was sixteen years old. Yet here she was. Who would have ever thought that she and Todd would be orphans living together in their parents' house? Todd, a dad raising a toddler. And both trying to be the best Christians possible? It had not been easy for either one of them, but especially hard on Todd.

That first year she had never seen him so down. Getting a divorce and moving back home had changed him in ways even the death of their mom and dad had not. Every time his ex-wife Caroline came up, she started to burn. What nerve. No sorry, no thought for the baby. It turned out she was running around on Todd. Yeah. Some surprise. Not. She tried to reign in her unkind thoughts. *The struggle is real. If I ever see her, I would just want to smack her.*

Todd had been on the phone with a friend of his and Caroline's from Seattle when he mentioned Caroline had moved to Oregon with her boyfriend. Jen had been hearing one side of the conversation as she did the dishes and looked over when Todd gasped. She saw him trying to hold it together. He hurriedly made an excuse to hang up.

"What?" Jenny had asked worriedly, looking at his ashen face. He hadn't answered at the time. He just shook his head and scooped up Tyler out of the highchair, leaving the room without a word.

When Jenny had looked in on them a little later, Tyler was asleep in Todd's arms, and Todd was just sitting at the window looking out on the mountains. His look had been so pained that Jenny had just quietly closed the door and left in tears.

She was hurt for those two guys. It took him a week to tell her what the problem had been.

"Good riddance," she mumbled, thinking through a million insults she would say to Caroline despite her best efforts.

Todd had clung to God through the whole ordeal, believing that He would bring some good out of it. There were always taped verses on the refrigerator when he was trying to memorize scripture, and the one he had chosen for that time stayed with Jenny too.

> Trust in the Lord with all your heart
> And lean not on your own under-
> standing. (Proverbs 3:5)

It was still on the refrigerator almost two years later as a reminder to them both that God was faithful.

She turned her attention back to Steve. "I'm sure it's okay," Jenny said, motioning for Steve to sit down. "Just let me run back and tell Maggie I'm here."

She was already pulling off her coat, hat, and gloves while swinging around the counter to toss her backpack in the cabinet. She scooted down the hall into the area they fondly called the den. The den was just an old closet space where they kept the computer plus coffee and pastry supplies.

Maggie was sitting on a stool with her head cocked at the computer screen, looking exasperated, face wrinkled in distaste. She had her ever present cup of coffee in her hand.

Maggie said it was her love of the stuff that made her open the café twenty years before. Of course, she always added, "Back then, you didn't have fancy-shmancy latte this and mocha that. You just brewed a pot of coffee and kept the customers' cups filled to the brim with steaming hot coffee." She always then shrugged her shoulders and said give them what they want. Customers, she would harrumph.

She was a good sport, short and plain with about thirty extra pounds to make her look huggable. She had the most amazing way of looking at you like she could see right through you, never judging, just kinda sizing you up, seeing what you were made of.

She had been like a mother to Jenny since she had lost her own mom. They had their differences to be sure; faith among the biggest, but she trusted Mag's to be tough but fair.

She was a widow. Her husband, Joe, had died a long time ago. Jenny never knew him, but he must have been something because the only time Maggie ever looked sad or vulnerable was when she spoke of her late husband. Then a wishful look would come into her eyes, and she would tell the girls stories after the shop closed, and they were all cleaning up about their courtship and marriage. Once, she looked up as Maggie spoke and saw the tears in her eyes. Her own eyes filled with tears. She got it.

She and Maggie shared an understanding of grief, an emotion that gets better but never really goes away.

If I could find a relationship half as good as Maggie and Joe or her parents, she thought wistfully, *a love that strong? What a blessing that would be.* Jenny brushed aside her thoughts with a frown.

"Man, I am getting a one-track mind," she muttered. "Too many romance novels—way, way too many romance novels."

Maggie looked up from the computer screen with a raised eyebrow. "Wadya say, hon?" she asked, distracted.

"Just wanted to let you know I was here. Is it okay if I take a few minutes to talk to Steve Baltyn?" She shifted impatiently from one foot to another.

"Steve, huh? By all means," she said with a knowing smile. "Who am I to get in the way of Mr. Wonderful nature boy?" She laughed at her own description.

Jenny's face burned. "Aw, Maggie, you know there's nothing between us, *at least, not until he's a Christian.*" She couldn't keep the note of wistfulness out of her voice, however.

"Just kidding ya, Jenny. Take as long as you need. If it's important and Dawn gets busy, although I can't imagine that happening as slow as it is, tell her to yell, and I'll come up front to give her a hand." Maggie smiled at her. "Do me a favor, will ya? Turn down the thermostat. Either I'm having a hot flash, which I thought I was done with, or it's getting warmer out."

Grinning Jenny was already closing the door and heading back to the front of the shop. "I'll check it, Mags. Thanks. You're the best!"

Jenny headed back to the front and pulled Dawn aside.

Dawn qualified as the friendliest person on the planet. She loved to talk to people. She was a tiny brunette with big brown eyes behind her glasses and shoulder length hair that she swore she hated. Sometimes Maggie had to gently remind her that she had let the coffee pot run over or a pastry burn in the toaster while she was immersed in conversation with someone who caught her interest at the counter. She could talk and talk about Alaska and the environment. She never wanted to move. She was going to stay forever. She was fond of telling her and anyone else that would listen that nobody had as beautiful a place to live in as they did.

"I'm going to be a few minutes okay, Dawn? Maggie said if you need help, just yell."

Dawn smiled unconcerned. "No problem. There's nothing going on. Nothing going on with work anyway," she said mischievously.

Jenny stuck out her tongue and headed for the table Steve was sitting at.

Jenny flopped into the seat next to Steve. "Sorry, I took so long. So what's up? Is everything okay? What did you want to talk to me about?" She realized she was babbling like an idiot. *I have no idea why he makes me so nervous*, she thought as she tried to stop talking.

Steve took a deep breath and stammered, "The thing is Jen…well, you're going to think I'm an idiot." Steve hesitated. "I just wondered…well…"

Now Jenny felt back in control and could be a little expansive. *Better help him out*, she thought. *Whatever's on his mind is obviously important to him.*

"*Yes?*" she prompted gently. That seemed to snap him back into the moment.

He tried again. "Well…here goes. I was wondering if you remembered what you said last summer—when you brought the youth group up to the center."

Jenny volunteered with the youth group at Abundant Life Church of God. They went on camping trips, retreats, and mission trips during the year. She enjoyed working with the teens, especially having been in their position not too long ago and trying to figure where Christ fit into her own life.

That day had been an enjoyable one. They had taken a group of fifteen kids to the Ketchikan Southwest Community Center, the tourist information, and learning center for the Tongass National Forest.

Steve worked as a ranger there, and he had given the group their tour. He had shared with them his passion for conservation and patiently answered the billion questions they asked. They ended the evening at nightfall around a safe campfire.

The kids had been taught how to pick up dead wood from a clearing rather than cut from living branches and how to ring the fire with stones to keep the fire contained. He also told them to have water or loose dirt handy in case of emergency, which he explained could happen quickly just by a shift in the wind.

The kids worked quickly at their assigned tasks until the fire was built and then sat roasting marshmallows, laughing and talking amongst each other. Jenny had taken a moment after the tour to compliment Steve on the day. She could tell the kids had really enjoyed themselves, and she was impressed, not only with how he treated the teens but also his knowledge of the forest.

They had a nice conversation, and Jenny had mentioned to him that he would be a great asset at church working with the kids. He had thanked her but didn't seem too interested in pursuing anything church related, and Jenny had let it drop.

Steve continued seeming at a loss for words, "You mentioned that day you thought I would be good working with the kids at your church." He looked at her and shrugged. Running his hand nervously through his hair, he raised an eyebrow and said, "Did you really think that, or were you just saying it?" He didn't wait for her to answer. "The thing is I can't get it out of my mind. I keep thinking about it—projects that would be great for them, places I could take them. I must have planned a whole summer's worth of stuff. I know it seems stupid because I don't even go to your church, but I can't believe how interested they all were. Aw, you probably think I'm crazy."

Her conscious kicked into high gear in that moment, and as it often happened, the Holy Spirit chided her gently. She should have known that God leaves nothing to chance. All this time, Steve had been feeling the tug of the Spirit, but Jenny had written him off. She had not one time lifted him before God and asked God to save him. She had not sent one prayer up to heaven on his behalf.

Jenny suddenly was very ashamed of her self-centeredness. It's one thing not to shove down someone's throat; it was quite another to forget about them completely.

"I don't think you're crazy," she said quietly. She leaned forward and said with all sincerity, "That was a great outing. You were really something with the kids. Some of our trips have been real busts. Man, they hate when people talk down to them, but we run into that all the time. People just have no patience with them. They are good kids though, and you seemed to see that right away. They responded to you too. I *do* think you would be great with them. Are you thinking about, um, coming to church?"

How do you phrase this? she thought, panicked for a minute. *Gee, Steve, did you get saved? Who made up that term anyway?* she thought, frustrated. *It makes it sound so, you know, condescending. Ugh!*

Steve looked at her unflinchingly.

"I was thinking about it, yeah…you know, my parents were Christians." He looked at her closely, trying to gauge her reaction.

Jenny looked at him surprised. Now this was an interesting piece of information. Jenny wanted to ask him a million questions, but she was cautious.

Everyone thinks they're Christian. People tossed out those words not even thinking about what it meant.

A Christlike life—it was not a religion to her. It was a relationship—one that she worked very hard on every day. Christian—that could mean something very different to him than it did to her.

She was about to launch into the subject when the bell from the door jingled, and Todd came in, holding Tyler by the hand. His little face was concentrated on his feet as he watched them with fascination. Or maybe it was the gym shoes he was wearing. They were that kind that lit up with red lights when he walked.

Tyler loved them. She had told Todd it was a wonder the baby had ever learned to walk properly, but Todd just laughed. Seeing the baby brought a smile to her face despite the fact that her brother, as usual, had terrible timing. He came over to the table, and as Tyler climbed into her lap, Todd raised his eyebrow ever so slightly at her with a meaningful look at Steve.

Great, she groaned in her head. She did not want to explain. Heck, what was there to explain anyway? *So far nothing has happened.* Oops, where did that *so far* come from? She shrugged it off and gave Todd her best fake smile—the "nothing going on here" smile she had perfected as the younger sister. She pulled off the baby's hat and coat while he wiggled around in her lap, wanting to get down.

Steve smiled at the baby, and he shook hands with Todd.

"Hey, Jenny, Steve. It's been awhile since I've seen you, Steve. How's everything?"

Jenny looked at him and sighed. Her brother was so good with people. They talked for a few minutes about Steve's job and Todd's job and the rumor that Eaglecrest Ski Resort might be expanding.

Everyone wanted to try the new snowboard run that was opening in two weeks. Jenny glanced at her watch and regretfully got up. She handed the baby to Todd.

"Sorry, guys, but I am way overdue to start. I don't want to take advantage of Mags."

Steve got up and said, "I have to run too. Um, maybe we can finish talking another time, Jenny?"

Jenny was sure the Lord whispered to her because suddenly, as clear as day, she heard that still small voice say *church* in her head. She started. It had been like someone standing next to her whispering in her ear. She impulsively shot out, "Yeah, actually, why don't we talk after church on Sunday? You could go to service and then come by the house. It's my turn to cook, and Todd won't care, right, Todd?" *He had better say yes,* she thought.

Todd looked surprised but nodded quickly, "Absolutely. You would love our church, and Jenny's learned a few things about cooking since I came back home with the baby."

Steve didn't hesitate. "I'd like that. So I'll see you guys at church then." He waved as he left.

Jenny stared after him, forgetting her brother for a minute.

Todd looked up at her and, with a speculative look at her, said in his big brother voice, "Now what exactly was *that* all about?"

Jenny snapped back to reality and stuck her tongue out at Todd. "He's coming to church, Todd."

Todd raised his eyebrow.

"We're just friends. I would do the same for anyone."

He smiled at that.

"I didn't come here for a big discussion about your love life." He coughed to hide his laugh. "I just came for a cup of coffee and to tell you that there is a letter at home for you from Laura." Todd was always hounding her to read Laura's letters. She gave him the ones that didn't have anything too personal for him to read. He thought Laura was a great friend for her to have. She could hear him saying, "Now *that* girl has a good head on her shoulders," while giving her one of his meaningful glances—glances that spoke volumes about the head he perceived she had on *her* shoulders.

Jenny raised her eyebrow and teased Todd right back, "I'm surprised you didn't steam it open, so you could be the first to read it."

With that parting shot, she walked back to the counter and started busying herself with some mugs that were in the sink. She knew Todd would bide his time and try for more information on Steve later. She sent a quick confused prayer up to the Lord. *I'm not sure what's going on here, Lord. Help me to be in Your will.*

She rushed through the day preoccupied, and before she knew it, closing time had come. She was wiping down the tables some kids from her youth group had been sitting at. She smiled; they were all so filled with energy and hope for the future.

They had so many plans. She had been like that a million years ago. Jenny thought for the first time in months, *I miss Mom.* She missed sitting at the table with a cup of coffee and talking about this or that.

Her mom always knew when something was bothering her or when she was feeling lonely. She was shocked to think it was coming up on five years that they had been gone. Five years! The time had gone so fast! So much had happened— good and bad: Todd finding God, the baby, the divorce. It seemed like they had lived a lifetime without their parents. *How could it be only five years?* she thought. *I was twenty-two. My god.* She shook herself free of the morose thoughts. Her parents had been a gift from God.

She looked up as Dawn threw herself into a seat at the table she was wiping down. Dawn swatted her with the dishrag she was holding. "You sure have been quiet today. Something going on with a certain somebody I should know about?"

Jenny groaned.

"It's obvious my life is so pathetic that everyone is look- ing for any signs of life. No, there is nothing going on, espe- cially if you're talking about Steve, and I know you are. He just wanted to ask about church or something."

Dawn looked surprised. "I didn't think he was one of you guys."

Her eyes grew big.

"Oh, I didn't mean that the way it sounded," she said hastily. "I just didn't think he was a church guy. You know, I think you're the greatest. Hey, doesn't that mean you two could get together?"

Jenny rolled her eyes.

Dawn was married to her high school sweetheart, Jeff, and was blissfully happy.

"Whoa, first of all, I don't think he has given his heart to the Lord yet. Secondly, I am not desperate. I am going to go with just anyone—Christian or not!" She knew she was sounding defensive, but she couldn't help it.

This day had started so promising, and now all she wanted to do was go home and fall into bed with a good book. She hated feeling like an old maid. You would think being single was a disease the way people were so sympathetic toward her, like she had a condition or something.

Truthfully, she didn't see all that many marriages that were so spectacular she would envy them anyway besides Dawn and Jeff who were so lovey-dovey. It was sickening or cute, depending on her mood she admitted ruefully. What was so great about fighting about money all the time or being so tired from the kids that you never spent any time with each other? She knew there were bunches of women in the church that were saved, but their spouse wasn't, and she felt the worst for them.

The Bible described a husband or a wife as a *helpmate*. That was how it was supposed to work. Each one had their own unique role.

However, so few couples were achieving that. She wondered what had happened to the power described in Acts. Where was the Holy Spirit? But just as quickly as the question formed, she knew the answer: Satan getting in and destroying families. It made sense. If Satan could pull down the families, he could cause damage that went on for generations. So many people had accepted the lie that marriage vows were temporary—at the first sign of trouble, they bailed. Jenny had seen the problems firsthand with the youth at church that came from broken homes, not to mention her own nephew who was being raised without his mom.

She shuddered to think what the great Jehovah thought about all this ungodliness and where had it gotten them. *Ugh!* She made a face and decided being single had its upside. If she ever did want to get married, the man would have to be a rock-solid man of God. She tried to explain it to Dawn who listened patiently.

"I guess I never thought about it like that, Jen," Dawn said. "I never think about Satan being, you know, like real." Her voice trailed off unsure.

Jenny responded fervently, warming to the subject, "He is, Dawn. Think about it. How many awful things happen? My parents, for example. That's not God. He lets people make their own decisions. Good or evil. If I choose to marry or let's just say date someone like Steve who's not saved, what am I letting myself in for? Will he understand why I want to be in church on Sunday instead of watching football or sleeping in? Will he understand when things are going wrong that we need to pray? Will he believe we need to tithe?"

Dawn interrupted her, "Tithe? What's that?"

Jenny replied, "That's the 10 percent of your income that you give to the church."

Dawn opened her mouth and sputtered, "You give 10 percent of your money to the church?" Disbelief was written all over her face.

Jenny, uncomfortable, said defensively, "Well, yeah. I didn't know what that meant at first either, but it makes perfect sense. How in the world is the church supposed to run if the members don't help? We have to have lights, right?"

Dawn nodded her head, silently agreeing.

"Well, it says in a bunch of places in the Bible to bring your tithe into the storehouse—the church it means—so that there might be meat in mine house or something like that. I don't have the exact words, but you see what I mean? Meat is just another way to say money. The church should always be able to function. I think I'm making it sound more complicated than it is." She sighed and said earnestly, "Someone who's not living by faith won't understand that. Even Christians sometimes have a hard time giving up their money. I tell you what, Dawn. Todd and I tithe on everything, and the more we give, the more we seem to have! I'm not kidding! It's amazing. But what guy is going to do that, trust like that if he doesn't know God and trust God like I do?" Jenny finished her speech with a shrug.

Dawn could take it or leave it, but she had lived most of her life without God and the last few years *with* God. She would take the last few years over the first twenty or so no problem.

"I guess it makes sense. It's a lot to think about," Dawn said hesitantly. "I didn't mean to upset you."

"No, it's not you," Jenny replied. "It's been a long day. I think I'm just ready to go home and crash."

"I'm with you on that," Dawn said, getting up and brandishing a towel. "Let's finish cleaning up."

She and Dawn hurried through the rest of the café in amicable silence, and she was glad that Dawn didn't hold grudges. She was pretty sure that she had made a mess of a simple conversation but reminded herself that there was grace for that!

When they finished, they both grabbed their coats and headed out. Jen flipped the sign to closed and locked the door.

CHAPTER *8*

. . . .

JENNY SEARCHED FRANTICALLY THROUGH the Sunday crowd. As usual, the auditorium was filled with people meeting and greeting each other, hugging and handshaking, and kids were running around the pews and then back downstairs to their Sunday school classes. Jenny tried not to look anxious, but her hopes were crashing down around her. Only a few more minutes until the service started, and still no sign of Steve.

So much for getting up an extra hour early to make sure her hair and makeup looked good, she sat down in a huff behind the teen pew and stewed. *I'm not going to let it get to me. I am not going to let this take away from my day of worship. This is God's day. Who cares about some stinking guy?* All the things that she usually told herself to cheer up were falling decidedly flat this morning.

The music started, and the teens needed a nudge to get to their feet, and by nudge she meant, she tapped the nearest one on the back of the head and motioned with her hand *get up*. Mission accomplished as the row reluctantly stood to their feet. She camouflaged a laugh by coughing, not wanting them to think their behavior was funny.

For the moment, Jenny forgot about Steve and lost herself in worship. With hands lifted toward heaven, she sang with all her heart, "Shout to the Lord." It was one of her favorite songs.

My Jesus, my Savior Lord, there is none like You
all of my days I want to praise the wonders of Your mighty love
My comfort, my shelter, tower of refuge and strength
Let every breath all that I am never cease to worship You
Oh! Shout to the Lord all the earth let us sing
Power and majesty, praise to the King
Mountains bow down, and the seas will
roar at the sound of Your name
I sing for joy at the works of Your hand.
Forever I'll love You, forever I'll stand
Nothing compares to the promise I have in You.

Jenny whispered a soft thank-you to the Lord and wiped a tear away as she opened her eyes. Steve was next to her in the pew, looking around at the people. Her heart started thumping wildly in surprise. He smiled at her as she stared at him staring at her. She flushed; her face aflame as she tried to compose herself.

"Hi," he said softly.

She smiled in return, unable to speak. That tugging in her heart was getting too strong to ignore, and it scared her.

She turned her eyes back to the front where the pastor was speaking, "We not only love God here, but we also love people. Turn to a few of your neighbors and greet them before you sit down."

Steve awkwardly hugged her and then turned to greet the people behind them. Jenny took a few minutes to hug the teenage girls in front of her and then turned back to her seat giving Steve a side glance. They both sat down at the same time, and Jenny sighed with relief because her legs were suddenly having a hard time holding her steady.

As Pastor Duffy preached, Steve leaned forward in the pew, listening intently. Jenny was torn between praying for what she didn't know, glancing at Todd, and trying to look casual and paying attention to the sermon, which she was sure she needed. She realized she had missed most of it, and by most, she meant all of it when she heard the pastor say, "Please bow your heads. No one looking around. This is a moment between you and God."

Jenny bowed her head, and with closed eyes, she listened as Pastor Duffy asked for a show of hands from those that were not where they ought to be in their walk with Jesus. Jenny always responded with an uplifted hand to that one because she didn't think you could get to the place where you didn't need to go any further. Then the pastor asked if anyone felt God calling them to a new life—salvation. Jenny peeked. She opened her eyes in the barest slit and tried to see if Steve lifted his hand. *I'm awful*, she thought, *or nosy. Both. Ugh. I'm both. I can't tell. Is his hand up? Please, God.*

The pastor acknowledged the hands and asked those who had raised them to come to the altar for prayer. Jenny was disappointed when Steve stayed seated.

A moment later, she whispered, "Excuse me," as she slipped out of the pew to pray with a young girl who was at the altar crying into her hands. She handed her some tissue that they kept at the altar for just such an occasion and gave her a hug and an encouraging smile. *So many kids hurting*, she thought. She didn't get back to her seat until the dismissal.

As she left the pew with Steve close by, she reminded herself again not to be disappointed and not to have such huge expectations. She caught Steve's eye and smiled. The two of them hung out by the door, waiting for Todd to finish up with a meeting he had to attend right after service. He promised to just be a minute, which in Church of God time was at least fifteen minutes.

Tyler was squirming in her arms, so she put him down and trailed after him as he wandered through the crowd. Jenny introduced Steve as people stopped to marvel at how big Tyler was getting and welcomed her guest. They chatted about this and that until she saw her brother heading her way. They stopped for a minute to get a plan together, and Steve decided he would tail along behind them in his own car to their house. She waited in the front seat as Todd put Tyler in his car seat and tried to look noncommittal. Bored even. Of course, considering Todd had watched in amazement as she flew around the house at the crack of dawn this morning, he was really being nice. He had not made one comment. Miraculous really.

Todd buckled in and turned slightly toward her. "Jenny," Todd said deliberately.

I know it was too good to last, she thought sourly. *Here comes the big brother act part one.* "Don't start, Todd," she said short and to the point. "Don't ruin this day for me. I don't know why it's important to me, but it is, and God will work it out, so there."

She knew she sounded like a child. *Why, oh, why*, she thought. *Does he always bring this out in me?* She took a deep breath to settle herself down and start looking out the window so she wouldn't have to look at him. She watched in the side mirror as Steve followed in his Jeep. He drove a Jeep Cherokee. Red.

Suits him, she thought.

The baby dropped off to sleep, and the adults maintained a semi-uncomfortable silence the rest of the way home. Jenny was busy with her own thoughts, and Todd knew he wasn't going to get anywhere if he didn't back off, at least for the moment. If she knew him, and she did, he was figuring that he would get a chance to talk to Steve some other time preferably when Jenny was too busy to notice. *Fat. Chance.*

*****

The lunch went off without a hitch. Steve sat around, having coffee with her and Todd until late. It was nice, comfortable even. Even her brother seemed relaxed.

Steve had listened to Todd talk about how tough it was to be a single dad but how the Lord had seen him through the bad times. Steve seemed impressed.

Jenny was just about to see if anyone wanted more coffee when she saw him glance at his watch. She looked at hers and couldn't believe it. Six already? "My gosh. I didn't realize I had overstayed my welcome like this. You guys won't want me back!"

Steve jumped off the couch and moved to grab his coat from the back of the chair where he had laid it.

"Don't be silly! It was fun," Jen exclaimed, hurriedly getting off the chair.

Todd was on his feet a moment later. "You're always welcome, Steve. We don't have enough people over, and I for one can get really sick of Jen's company."

Jen shot him a murderous glare.

He shook Steve's hand. "I'll just go get Tyler down for the night. Seriously, you're welcome anytime."

Jen headed for the door behind Steve while Todd headed upstairs.

"Thanks again for the invitation, Jen. It was a really good day." Steve tucked his hands into his pockets and looked at her expectantly.

"I was so glad you came. It was fun." Jen shifted awkwardly from one foot to the other. "Anytime you want to come to church, please come."

"Oh yeah. I will. Okay, thanks again." He turned away, tugging the keys out of his pocket.

Jen watched him until he got into the car and then waved shutting the door. Leaning back on the door, she took a deep breath. No hug, no kiss—nothing to indicate a romance, but Jenny felt something there. She could see the Lord working on his heart, and she needed to be careful that she didn't jeopardize that for her own needs.

She shook her and started up the stairs to bed, but she had a feeling she was going to have a hard time going to sleep. Changing into her pajamas, she restlessly wandered around her room not feeling like reading or watching TV.

She finally tiptoed into Tyler's room. She watched his little chest rise and fall in regular breaths. He was so beautiful. She wouldn't admit it if someone asked, but she used to stand over Tyler when he first came, worried that he would stop breathing. She would finally drag herself away when she couldn't keep her eyes open any longer and drag herself back to her own room. Where the paranoia came from, she had no idea. Maybe it was as simple as she just wasn't used to having babies around or her parents not being there for support. Or the fact that his mom had deserted him. He seemed so fragile. She couldn't love him more if she had given birth to him herself of that she was sure.

She heard Todd closing up the house downstairs. He must have been working late at his computer. She made her way back to her own bed and drifted off to the sound of his feet coming up the stairs, making her feel safe and protected.

The phone ringing jolted her awake. She looked over at the clock. It was 3:00 a.m. Her brain was still fuzzy, but alarms started to go off. *Has something bad happened?* Her body instantly flashed on the night she got the call about her parents being killed.

Nausea made her stomach churn. With a sick feeling and her heart thudding, she made her way quickly out of her room. She could hear Todd's voice rising in anger, drawing her down the hall to his room. She stopped outside the door surprised when she heard him say, "Caroline, you're sounding crazy. Have you been drinking?"

Caroline? They hadn't heard a peep from her in ages. What could she be calling for this late?

Jenny's senses were coming awake fast. Maybe she had been out partying. She could hear Todd's voice getting snappish. She wondered if she should just go back to bed or pop her head in to make sure everything was okay. She didn't want to intrude. On the other hand, Caroline had caused a lot of pain for this family, which had already had more than its fair share.

Todd's tone caused a shudder to run through her. She bit her lip torn between staying and going.

"What! That will never happen! Never. Do you hear me? Don't call here again, Caroline!" Todd was really shouting, which he never did anymore, and the slamming phone echoed through the hall. This was serious. She knocked and stuck her head in gingerly. He was up and pacing the room.

"Todd, you okay? What did Caroline want?"

He looked at her and snorted.

"She said she missed Tyler. She thinks he needs to be with her."

Jenny gasped.

"She was drunk. It didn't mean anything. I don't even know why I let her get to me." He was trying to calm down now; she could see him taking deep breaths.

"She can't do that, right, Todd?" Jenny wanted to hear it was impossible. Impossible.

He smiled a shaky smile that did not reach his eyes. "She can't do that," he stated.

Just to hear him say so relieved her. Of course, she couldn't take Tyler away. Tyler didn't even know his mother. Not that Todd had ever tried to keep her away, she had just never bothered. She did something she hardly ever did.

She walked into the room and hugged her brother. "I love you, Todd." She smiled as his eyes welled up. "It will be okay. We've been through worse. We'll figure it out in the morning. Don't let her get to you. Go to bed."

Todd took another long breath. She watched him exhale in a long whoosh. "I will as soon as my blood pressure goes back to normal. Thanks. I'm okay. I shouldn't have let my temper get the best of me. Caroline just took me by surprise. I'm okay."

Jen didn't really think that repeating it was making it so, but she nodded like she agreed with Todd. "Yup. All right. Well, if you need me, just wake me up."

She made her way to her room. She was definitely not as calm as she pretended for Todd. Her heart was still racing, and her hands were shaking.

"Protect them, Lord," she whispered from her heart.

Finally dozing off an hour later, she slept worse than she ever had. Waking up cranky and out of sorts, Jenny made her way slowly to her desk. She picked up the letter she had half-heartedly written to Laura the other day. She had toyed with the idea of going to Trinidad just for a change of pace, but Trinidad seemed very far away, and somehow, she just didn't feel right about it. She kept putting it off and wondered if it had anything to do with liking Steve.

She sat at the desk and waited on the Lord. Something quiet spoke that morning. She just knew that it was not God's plan for her to go to Trinidad just now. She sighed. *That's probably why I couldn't finish the letter*, she thought. *Laura will understand. She is the one person I can count on to not make me feel guilty, especially if I feel it's God working in some way.*

She took her time writing out her thoughts for Laura, sealed the letter, and went down to the kitchen.

By 10:00 a.m., she was throwing a load of clothes in the washing machine, singing to her favorite tunes from Hillsong UNITED when the ringing phone broke into her thoughts. For one sickening moment, she hesitated, wondering if it was Caroline again. *She wouldn't dare call back after Todd yelling at her like that though, would she?*

She picked up the phone deliberately, cheerful just in case. If it was Caroline, she didn't want her to think they were worried. "Hello!"

"Wow, are you always this cheerful in the morning?" Steve asked.

Thrown off guard, Jenny stumbled over a reply and then fell silent. *What the heck is the matter with me?* she thought.

Steve filled in the silence.

"I wanted to say thanks again to you and your brother for yesterday. I had a really good time," he hesitated. "Look, um, I was wondering if you wanted to go skiing on Friday? If you don't have to work, I mean?"

What to do? What to do? Jenny flashed on all the times she had told her teen class not to date unsaved people. How it would just lead to problems. She had been adamant with her take on it that it was a black-and-white issue. No room for compromise. Served her right.

She didn't know what to say. Well, she knew *what* to say; she just didn't know how to say it. She couldn't go. She couldn't be that kind of hypocrite. It was a date, right? She wanted to go so bad.

"Steve, it's not that I don't want to," she hesitated, "but I don't think it would be a good idea."

"Oh, well, um, no problem. Just checking."

"It's not that I don't want to!" Jenny said, rushing to explain. "It's just that I have this thing about dating someone who is not a part of the church. Like, um, one because I work with teens, and two, well, it's a personal belief that when you're looking for a husband…" *Oh my god, did I just say I was looking for a husband!* "I mean, I'm *not* looking for a husband. Well, I'm not, not looking for a husband." Jenny went silent. "Steve, can I, um, call you later?" *God does that sound as awful to him as it does to me? I feel hot. Is it hot in here?*

"Sure thing. I'll, um, talk to you later then. Um, bye."

The line went dead. Obviously, it did sound that awful to him. Jenny collapsed, face burning into the kitchen chair totally defeated. Her mind was blank. She was still sitting there an hour later when Todd came in. He looked a little worse for the wear himself. She knew just how he felt. Her problems were small in comparison to what he had to deal with, but she was disappointed and embarrassed.

"Hey, Jen, what's up?" he asked, looking at her strangely.

She shrugged her shoulders.

"If it's about last night, I told you don't worry about it. Caroline didn't mean anything. She was drinking. Probably just a whim. She might not even remember it today," he spoke reassuringly.

She gave him a half-hearted smile. "I know. It's not that. I…I…uh, talked to Steve this morning. He called to say thanks for dinner."

Todd waited for more. "And?" he prompted.

Jenny looked at him blankly. "Nothing," she whispered, withdrawing into a shell. Throwing the last of the clothes she had been mindlessly folding on the table into the basket, she pulled herself out of the chair and drifted out of the room.

CHAPTER 9

....

TODD SHIFTED TYLER IN his arms, trying to keep him occupied and still listen to the man behind the desk. "So you think I'm right to take this seriously?" Todd asked hesitantly.

Larry Landon leaned forward in his chair. He was a small man, only 5'6" and less than 150 lbs. He had intense brown eyes and a friendly, encouraging smile. He pushed back his curly hair that always fell across his forehead, making him look slightly disheveled, and replied earnestly, "I don't think threats like this should be ignored."

Todd paled visibly at the use of the word *threat*. He had come into this appointment, hoping to have his fears put to rest. It was just not going to happen. *Oh, God*, he prayed silently, *Where are You? Give me wisdom.*

Suddenly, he felt so alone. He looked at Mr. Landon—Larry rather—as he had said to call him right away. He liked him. He had instantly put him and Tyler at ease, coming around the desk to speak directly to the toddler, who had looked at him with big solemn brown eyes.

Finally, he coaxed a smile out of him by offering him a sucker. But this was serious business, and frankly, Todd wished he had never had to come here. "I just don't know what to do. What the next steps should be?" Todd shrugged helplessly.

"I understand, Todd. You leave this to me. This is my area of expertise. Hey, if everyone could do it, we wouldn't need lawyers, right? I'm going to walk you through what we are going to do now."

Leave it to him. Todd wanted to leave it to him, to God, to anyone who could and would help him. Who could make it all go away? He had to constantly remind himself that God was in control. What had his mom always told him? "Fake it till you make it." He would fake this calm until it became a reality or until he got an ulcer.

Larry called his secretary in to take Tyler from Todd while they got down to business. The next two hours were spent going over the years prior to Tyler being born all the way to the present.

Todd recounted the lack of care for the baby and Caroline walking out. He told Larry about his move home. He answered questions that were painful and probing. Many times, he had to pause while Larry waited patiently for him to compose himself.

When he spoke of Christ and the profound effect God had on his life, Larry lifted an eyebrow but didn't comment. He just listened and wrote notes until Todd was exhausted and fighting a killer headache. Seeing his client had had enough for the day, Larry called a halt to the note taking, "We'll leave off here. This gives me a good start."

Larry noted that Todd didn't look too good. He really felt for the guy. It had been rough on him. He promised himself that he would take extra care not to let this one sit on the back burner too long. He had a feeling this Caroline was going to pull something, and he intended to be ready for her.

CHAPTER *10*

. . . .

STEVE SPENT THE AFTERNOON out in the yard, splitting logs for the fireplace, kicking himself for calling Jenny like that. He blew into his hands, trying to warm up, thinking the cold was only what he deserved. *What am I thinking?* he groaned. *I am a complete idiot. Someone like Jenny isn't going to be interested in me. She was so strong, and had been through so much. She was beautiful and smart and—* He broke off his thoughts with a rueful smile. He sounded like a lovesick cow. Where were these feelings coming from anyway? He had so much going on inside of him as it was. He had never felt so confused in his life. All of the sudden, his world seemed wrong. He was feeling like something was missing. If God was real and trying to reach him, he wanted to know.

He thought about praying, but it had been so long. He had to know, though once and for all if God was real or not. Needed to know if his parents and Jenny and everyone like them were just naive or if it was something more.

He heaved the ax up and over his head, gratified to hear the resounding thunk of the split wood. *What's next, Steve?* His breath puffed out visible in the cold air. He put the ax down and looked up. "Lord, I know it's been a while. A long while. I don't even know where to begin, but can You show me you're real? Can You help me to figure out what's next?"

Steve stared up at the sky for a few moments and then shook his head. "Okay then."

Gathering up a load of the wood to bring in for the fireplace, he thought about the conversation he and Jenny had the day her youth group came for the tour. He hadn't been able to get it out of his head. The more he thought about it, the more he had wanted to see her. One thing had led to another until yesterday: going to church, going to her house, sitting around with her and Todd.

It had been the nicest time he'd had since he moved here. *And now I've gone and ruined it.*

She wasn't interested in him as anything but a friend. He shouldn't have pushed her by asking her out, but looking at her last night as she made dinner, sitting with her on the couch talking, he had been stirred in a way no other girl had stirred him, interested in her as a person, as a woman. She had the qualities a man wanted in a wife: faithful, kind. It didn't hurt that she was beautiful on top of it—beautiful inside and out.

I have to fix this, he thought suddenly. *I don't want to lose her.*

Freezing, he dumped the wood into his storage box and hurried into his house. He was going to pray again, really try this time. He had the feeling God was listening and speaking, but he needed to figure out how to hear Him. He would be careful with Jenny. She deserved the best. He would just have to figure out how to be the best!

CHAPTER 11

WINTER TURNED TO SUMMER, and Jenny felt better than she ever had. The coffee shop was getting fuller by the day with the summer season starting and tourists filled with excitement over being in Alaska who were coming in every day exclaiming over the town and the wildlife.

The light infused everyone with energy. It reminded her of how heaven might be. Light all the time, except *that* light would be coming from God.

Everyone perked up. It was contagious. The only thing not going anywhere was her still strained friendship with Steve. He had been faithfully coming to church and had started attending Bible study on Wednesday nights a few weeks back. If anyone cared to look, there was real growth happening there. Not that anyone was looking or hoping or praying.

Jenny smiled as she made the rounds of the tables at the shop, cleaning up empty coffee cups and stacking them behind the counter to wash. She was keeping a secret from Todd. Laura was coming back home for a visit—July 1. Jenny would be picking her up at the ferry and driving her back to the house to stay for two whole weeks!

There was the church picnic on the Fourth of July with boating and food and games, which was always one of the greatest events of the summer. She had a feeling her brother was more interested than even he knew in Laura, and Jenny thought that perhaps a little matchmaking was in order.

Hey, if Laura and Todd get married, Laura would be family!

She continued down that road of thought giving her imagination free reign. *Gee, Laura and Todd could have a family. I would be an aunt again! It's so hard not to look ahead and dread her leaving before she even gets here,* Jenny thought— one of her many bad habits she needed to work on. A verse popped into her head.

> Take therefore no thought for the morrow: for the morrow shall take thought for the things of itself. Sufficient unto the day is the evil thereof. (Mathew 6:34)

Funny how she could never remember a verse when she wanted to, but when she wasn't thinking about verses at all, there it was. She could remember it word for word and exactly where it was in the Bible. *God sure does know what I need exactly when I need it.* She smiled.

*****

Jenny looked out the big picture window to the street and winced. "Dawn, can you make an iced vanilla latte for that woman that just left? Her daughter just knocked it over!"

The bear bells on the door chimed as the woman covered in coffee made her way to the counter with her young daughter firmly in hand. Jenny and Dawn exchanged a smile.

"We saw you had a little accident," Jenny said to the woman. "We're making you a new latte on the house."

The woman smiled gratefully, "Thanks so much!"

The little things. A free coffee. A smile. Jenny made a pact with herself then and there to enjoy Laura and not think about her leaving at all. She was definitely going to be a matchmaker, but she would leave it to God to furnish the results.

She was rather proud of herself and her self-control. She was still patting herself on the back when Steve came in with one of her friends from church—Eileen.

Eileen was beautiful, nice, and not of the same belief as Jenny that you shouldn't date people that don't have a relationship with God. Instantly, she was on edge. Eileen was in the same Bible study as Steve, and she knew they had become good friends.

She wrinkled her nose. "I think I'm going to be sick," Jenny muttered under her breath. She was staring at the table Steve and Eileen now occupied. *They look mighty chummy,* she thought darkly.

They sat down at one of the tables she was responsible for. *What a surprise. Why wouldn't it be? God's testing me. That's what it is. God's testing me. No, wait, it's Satan. Satan is tempting me. Yeah, that's it...an attack. Well, take this, Satan. I am not going to let this bother me.*

Dawn came up to her and whispered, "You better go wait on them, or it's gonna look funny. Do you want me to take the table?"

Jenny jumped. "No, I got it. Thanks though."

She threw down the dish towel she had been wringing the life out of and walked up to their table smiling brightly. Very, very brightly.

"Hiya, Steve, Eileen, what can I get you guys?"

Steve looked up quickly with a smile and then looked away. He seemed distracted, like he didn't even know she existed. Jenny felt a headache coming on. Clueless man.

"Hi, Jenny, I'm going to have a bagel toasted with cream cheese and a regular coffee." He put the menu down and looked at Eileen.

"I'll have plain toast and a tall skim latte. Thanks, Jenny." Eileen turned her attention back to Steve as Jenny beat a hasty retreat muttering, *I'll have a tall skim latte, and who eats plain toast, for God's sake?*

Jenny glanced over her shoulder at them as she put two slices of toast in the toaster and saw that they were deep in conversation. She shrugged her shoulders as she pulled the toast out of the toaster. *Whatever.* It took a few minutes, but she pasted the smile back on her face.

"Here ya go guys. Let me know if you need anything else."

They thanked her politely, barely looking up.

Must be important. None of my business. She glanced back at the counter to see Dawn giving her a sympathetic look. *I don't care. I don't care. I don't care. Ugh.* Funny how just when you think you have everything under control, you get sucker punched.

Steve and Eileen left an hour later, leaving Jenny to her very dark thoughts. She couldn't seem to help herself. She snapped at Dawn when she asked if she was okay.

"Why wouldn't I be!" she said then wanted to die for sounding so churlish. The more she tried to talk herself out of it, the worse it got.

You are being ridiculous. Stop being stupid. If God wants me to be with someone, if He really wants me to be with someone, it will happen. Why can't I believe that? Shouldn't I believe that?

She noticed Dawn escaped her mood by staying as far away as possible from Jenny the rest of the longest day ever.

When Jenny got home, she slammed the door behind her. She almost ran into Todd who was standing there like a statue.

JENNY

"Do you mind?" she spit out. She was moving toward the stairs when Todd reached out and grabbed her arm. She was so surprised she almost tripped. She was ready to start on a tirade when she realized how white his face was. Something was wrong. She looked at him again.

"Todd, what's wrong? Are you sick?"

He looked at her but didn't answer.

"Todd, you're scaring me. Are you okay?" she was trying to sound calm.

He handed her the letter he had been clutching in his hand. She could hardly open it; her hands were shaking so bad. She was not good with emergencies ever since her parents. Her body just immediately went into hyper mode at the thought of a problem.

Calm down, she told herself sternly.

She finally got the paper opened and in her hand. She read it, not understanding, and then read it again.

Custody of minor named herein—
Caroline Milner—
Requested to appear—

What the heck? Her face flushed with the realization of what she was holding. *That witch!* She looked at Todd's stricken face.

"Oh, Todd. Don't worry. It will be okay," she spoke in her most soothing voice.

He was shaking his head.

Well, at least, that was some response.

She spoke again in measured tones, getting him to focus on her, "Todd, listen to me. You have to get a lawyer. Do you know where you can get a lawyer?"

That seemed to snap him out of it. He looked at her sadly. He shook his head faintly in the affirmative, the move seeming to take all his energy, and said, "I talked to one the day after she called. Do you remember that night? I didn't think I would need him. I hoped I wouldn't need him. I hoped she would just lose interest like she always does. I didn't think she would go through with it…" His voice trailed off.

Jenny prompted him quickly, "What's his name, Todd? Where's his number? I'll call him for you."

Jenny was busy pulling him into the kitchen and pushing him into a chair as he pulled the card out of his wallet. "I'll take care of it." She was already picking up the phone. She squinted at the card, holding the phone to her ear. Larry Landon. "Hello, may I speak with Larry Landon please?"

THE NEXT DAY FOUND them both sitting in the law offices of Larry Landon. After a frantic call from Jenny, Mr. Landon had cleared his schedule the next afternoon and told them to come in. The ride into town was quiet. The only noise was Tyler talking to himself in the back seat.

Jenny liked Larry right off the bat. He spoke bluntly and to the point, and he was definitely on Todd's side. She tried not to look concerned as she listened diligently to all the options Larry was explaining to Todd. She figured he hadn't gotten much sleep last night and may need her to explain this all to him when they got home. They had Tyler with them. The idea of a babysitter watching him had become unacceptable, and without saying a word to each other, they included him.

Larry was leaning toward them reassuringly. "She really doesn't have a chance of gaining full custody," Larry said calmly. "But the possibility exists that the court would allow her some type of visitation. She never signed away her parental rights, and although her abandonment of Tyler doesn't look good, they tend to give parents a lot of leeway. Judges don't want to take away parental rights unless there is some kind of abuse. Even then if they go through court mandated counseling and parenting classes, they can get their kids back."

Jenn saw Todd visibly relax. So Tyler was not going to get ripped from his arms and never given back.

"So what the court will probably have us do is work out some kind of joint custody?" Todd asked.

Larry was shaking his head affirmatively as he answered, "That's the normal course. You don't have any reason to think that Tyler would be in danger in her company, do you? Because if that's the case, we can try to get her parental rights taken away. It would be a much longer process. A lot uglier too." He calmly waited for Todd to process that.

"No, nothing like that," Todd answered quickly. "It's just that she was never around. She never seemed interested in the baby. I wouldn't have stopped her from seeing him. She just never bothered."

Jenny thought he was being a tad generous and jumped in quickly. "When she called, she was drunk. How do we know she isn't drunk all the time?"

Larry referred to his notes. "Right, right. I remember Todd going over that," he said as he sat back in his chair. "You two go home, and I will file the countermotion, and when the judge sets a court date for the preliminary hearing, I'll give you a call."

They all stood up and moved toward the door.

"Try not to think about it. Just keep to your regular schedules. If Caroline tries to contact you, you don't speak with her. Just refer her to me. The less contact you have with each other, the better. Understood?"

They both nodded.

"Okay then, expect to hear from me by the end of the week."

CHAPTER *13*

. . . .

THINGS HAD BEEN MISERABLE around the house for weeks now. Jenny never got around to telling her brother that Laura was coming. He was so preoccupied she never found the right time to tell him. So now here, she was on the way to the ferry to pick up Laura who was blissfully unaware that anything was amiss. She never mentioned the custody problem because she wasn't ready to deal with it herself.

"Grief," she muttered to herself. "How do I get myself into these messes?"

She parked on the street and went down to watch for the ferry. Standing with her hip pressed against the wooden exit gate, she sipped her iced tea and peered at the water, waiting for the first glimpse of the ferry. She was so excited she was finally going to get to see her.

It had been such an emotional couple of weeks. She had been trying to make sure Tyler and her brother were okay and fretting about Laura coming in. She was thinking about Steve so often she wondered if she would ever get through a day without thinking of him again. It would be a relief to be able to get Laura's opinion on everything. Plus, in the back of her mind, she knew it would be good for Todd.

*****

The ferry was pulling in, and Jenny waved and shouted at Laura who was standing on the top deck waving back just as ent' isiastically.

It felt like it took forever for the boat to dock and allow Laura to get off. She bounced down the gangplank, pulling her carry-on with a backpack bumping against her hip as she moved toward Jenny. She was small and dark with short brown hair. She moved toward Laura quickly and enveloped her in a big hug!

"I'm so glad you're here!" Jenny exclaimed for the first time, realizing how desperately she had wanted Laura to be here.

Laura's eyes sparkled as she stepped back and looked at Jenny.

"You haven't changed at all," Laura said, affecting a fake disgusted tone. "It is completely unacceptable that you are so pretty."

Jenny snorted. "Don't get me started. I look like death warmed over, and I know it." She had bags under her eyes from too many sleepless nights worried about the future, worried about Tyler, worried about Todd, worried about Steve. If worry was a sin, and she thought it just might be, she was in terrible spiritual shape. They looked happily at each other, and Jenny finally started pulling her toward the car.

"C'mon, I have a million things to tell you and a million things to show you. Is that all you brought?" Jenny chattered happily as she tugged at Laura and moved off toward the car.

Laura's bag clattered on the wooden sidewalks until suddenly Jen realized Laura was not right behind her. She had stopped dead in her tracks ten feet behind her.

"What are you doing!" Jenny laughed.

"It's just been so long since I've been back!" Laura said. "I didn't even realize I missed it. I mean, the beaches in Trinidad and Tobago are pretty nice even if I don't get much time off to enjoy them, but this, oh, it just smells like heaven."

"Don't rub it in about the beaches. You know, I have a warm-weather beach obsession! It's summer now, so I'm fine, but come, winter, I will not like you one bit!"

They laughed together as if no time had passed since high school.

They stopped at Jenny's beat-up Volkswagen and tossed the bags in the back.

"Do you want to stop at Maggie's?" Jenny halted in her tracks, wondering out loud. "Do you even drink coffee? I never thought to ask before. Isn't that weird? That just never came up. You left junior year, and I don't think I was a big coffee person then?" her voice trailed off bemused.

Laura laughed again. "I do drink coffee. I would kill for some coffee right now. I also love a good cup of tea."

"Perfect!" Jenny exclaimed, slamming the car door. "Maggie's it is!"

*****

The bear bells over the door chimed their arrival. Maggie had put up the bear bells as a joke. The tourists always seemed to carry the big metal bells as a bear deterrent. No one told them they didn't work.

Every tourist shop on the street sold those at $10 a pop. Besides, it was, for the most part, harmless. Most people would never come close enough to a bear to worry about it.

Dawn came out from behind the counter and gave them both a hug. "I'm so glad to meet you, Laura. Jenny has told me a lot about you." Dawn smiled warmly. "Maggie is out but will be back soon."

When Jenny went to move behind the counter, Dawn shooed her away. "Sit down, for Pete's sake! I'll get you what you want. Do you want Laura to think we don't know how to treat our guests?"

"Technically, Laura is not a guest, Dawn," Jenny said tartly. "She *was* raised here even if her family did move!"

"Okay. How about you sit down anyway?" Dawn replied. "And treat your friend—you're probably very tired friend with some hospitality then?" Dawn stuck out her tongue at Jenny, setting the three of them into gales of laughter.

Wiping her eyes, Laura exclaimed, "Tired is right. I think I'm getting punchy. I haven't laughed like this in ages!" She squeezed Jenny's hand. "I really needed this!"

Dawn came back with the coffee, and after hanging around looking like she had a million questions she wanted to be answered, Jenny laughingly waved her into an empty seat. "Just sit down ya goof!"

"All right, but just for a minute." Dawn swept the floor with a look to see if anyone needed anything and sat down in the seat.

Maggie's was pretty busy. June started the high season, and July was the peak when things were in full swing. Tourists packed the place from the cruise ships and travelers coming in from day trips got coffee to go so they could walk the historic downtown and take in the scenery.

The girls happily spent an hour getting acquainted. Dawn would pop up to tend to customers and then sit back down, resuming the conversation.

Laura stifled a long yawn. "I am so sorry! Go on with what you were saying," Laura said.

"Oh my god, Laura!" Jenny exclaimed. "You have to be wiped! You look like you're going to fall over! I am so sorry! We should get you back to my place." Jenny had just noticed that Laura was having a hard time focusing.

"I have to admit I am fading fast. It just kinda hit me!" Laura responded.

"You guys get going," Dawn said. "Hopefully, I will see you guys tomorrow?"

"Yup," Jenny replied. "We are going to stop for coffee before we do any shopping."

"It was nice to meet you, Dawn," Laura said warmly, giving her a big hug. "We will see you tomorrow apparently!"

Jenny ushered her out the door in another chime of bear bells, into the car, and home to the spare bedroom in record time. Jenny looked in on her around dinner time, but she was still sound asleep, having crashed in the clothes she had been wearing, so she went downstairs to get something ready for dinner for the boys. Todd would be walking in any minute, and she wanted the surprise to go well. No better surprise than her cooking on a night that wasn't assigned to her.

She laughed to herself, "I just wish I had a camera to take a picture of his face when I tell him who's here."

She put some water on to boil, and before she knew it, the baby came walking in with his arms up wanting to get picked up. She had just put the spaghetti on, and she scooped him into her arms, drinking in his scent.

"Hey, bug," she said, making him giggle. She twirled him around, and he laughed.

Todd was right behind Tyler headed for the stove. "Hey, what's this? Isn't today my day to cook?" He sniffed appreciatively in the air. "Hey, whose bags are by the door?" he asked offhandedly.

"Oh, those are Laura's," she replied casually, watching his face for recognition, but he was busy putting Tyler in his highchair.

"Laura who? Laura Giles from church? Is she going somewhere?" He looked up quickly in a panic. "Did I forget that I'm supposed to take someone to the airport or ferry? I've been distracted."

Jenny took pity on him. She hadn't meant to cause him to panic, for goodness' sake.

He was already in such a state every day. Last week, she found the iron in the refrigerator. That had caused her to raise an eyebrow, but she had just taken it out and put it back with the ironing board without telling him what he had done.

I'm a good sister, she thought to herself.

He was totally panicking.

She waved her hand in front of his face. "Yoo-hoo anybody there? Earth to Todd. Those aren't Laura Gile's bags."

He looked at her blankly. "Oh." He stared at her. "Well, who's Laura then?" He looked completely baffled.

"They are Laura Tolliver's." She watched his face.

It took him longer than she thought it would. Her big brother was getting slow. Finally, she saw the recognition on his face, disbelief followed by something that she couldn't quite identify grazing the surface. Then a big grin. "Ya don't say now. How did you manage this little surprise?" He seemed duly impressed.

Jenny couldn't usually keep a secret. Jenny saw him look around at the table. It was just set for them.

"Well, where is she?" he asked.

Jenny grinned. "She was sound asleep when I checked on her, and I didn't want to wake her up. We stopped at Maggie's earlier, and she almost fell asleep on the table."

"Oh." His disappointed tone set Jenny's heart soaring. She was *so* going to make this match work!

Brother and sister looked at each other. They both grinned from ear to ear.

"Cool!" Todd exclaimed.

They dug into dinner with enthusiasm, laughing and talking and interrupting each other about who was going to show what to Laura, fighting good-naturedly about schedules, favorite places, forgetting about Caroline and custody for the first time in a long time.

The Southeast Alaska Visitors' Center was a definite must, and it was within walking distance of the cruise ship dock, which Jenny insisted she would want to see—the Ketchikan Museum on Dock Street.

The ideas flew back and forth as they tried to look at the town with the eyes of a tourist. Laura had not been back since graduation from high school when her family had moved to Utah, and Ketchikan had grown a lot. Floatplane rides were out; they figured too expensive for Laura, but they could all rent bikes in town. Kayaking—they weren't sure about. Having been raised in Alaska, they were both very active in sports but had no idea if Laura still was, so that was a wait and see.

Todd was going to tell the guys at the paper he was taking a few hours here and there to hang out, which they reasoned he could easily turn into a story and thus be working. "That was one good thing about being a newspaper man," he joked.

Everything was a potential story, so he had a lot of leeway when it came to his activities. Jenny knew it was going to be a great two weeks!

CHAPTER 14

··

LAURA WOKE UP WITH a headache and did not want to move. She stretched out first one limb then another, groaning when her muscles revolted against her. She felt like she had been run over. She was cold too, which was odd she thought considering it was usually 95 degrees and humid. She sat up suddenly, almost fainting as the blood rushed to her head. *Oh my gosh!* She wasn't in Trinidad; she was in Alaska!

Despite her aches and pains, she leapt out of bed and ran to the bedroom window. Happy memories of sleepovers and friends came rushing back.

Jenny's house was set back off a dirt road surrounded by pines. She barely remembered anything from after Maggie's as they drove up the night before. She had been so tired.

They were surrounded by trees. *It smells wonderful!* She craned her neck first one way than another, trying to see everything. Her eyes opened wide as something skittered away into the trees.

"Okay. It's been a long time since I've dealt with more than an iguana," she muttered under her breath. *I'm not sure about walking around here.*

Her family, when she was growing up, had lived in an apartment in town. Jenny's house was twenty minutes outside of town and was like the other side of the moon.

She looked around the room—her home for the next two weeks. It was super homey. There were wood floors softened by a bright floor rug done in an orangey kind of color that reminded her of the sunsets back home. The walls were bare except for a mirror over the dresser, but a cheery vase of flowers Jenny must have placed there looked and smelled wonderful. She looked around for a clock but didn't see one. She had no idea what time it was, and her phone was nowhere to be found, but she thought she should go looking for Jenny and not waste another moment of her visit.

She headed downstairs and found her way to the kitchen. She hesitated in the doorway where a man was sitting at the table scrolling through his phone. *This must be Todd*, she thought. *He's even cuter than I remember from school. Oh, the crush I had on him.* Suddenly, she didn't know what to do. She hung back, biting her lip when abruptly Todd looked up and right into her eyes.

"Hey," he said excitedly. He pushed back his chair and stood.

She fixed a smile on her face and remembered her manners. "Hey, Todd." She extended her hand.

Todd looked taken aback but quickly recovered and shook her hand vigorously. "Hey. It's been a long time. Are you hungry?" Todd asked. "I could make you some eggs or something. Jenny just took Tyler for a little walk outside to settle him down. She'll be right back." He gestured at the stove, which still contained the remnants of his own breakfast.

Laura was so startled by this offer she didn't immediately reply. She had never had a man cook for her in her whole life. Her mother did the cooking for her family, and if her mom didn't, then she was expected to.

Movement at the door saved her. Jenny walked in with Tyler who was holding out a branch for his father's inspection. Jenny ran to Laura and gave her a big hug. Laura hugged her back, relief written all over her face.

"I'm so glad you're up!" Jenny exclaimed. She continued on without a breath. "Did you sleep okay? Are you hungry?" she prattled on happily. The tension in the air evaporated as quickly as it had come.

Laura replied, laughing completely at ease with Jenny, "I slept soundly. Thank you. Where did you get that mattress topper? It was unbelievable. I want one for home, and yes, I'm starving!"

Jenny waved her into a chair. Todd held up the coffee pot. "Anyone?"

Jen nodded her head yes, and Laura, taking her cue from her, also nodded yes.

"Don't you love those pillow top mattress things? I ordered that one from Amazon. When they had a sale, I bought them for all the beds."

"I loved it. I will have to tell my mom about it," Laura replied.

Sitting with her hands curled around her coffee, Laura was entertained by the brother-sister duo who were bantering back and forth.

Todd served her a plate of eggs and toast, and she continued to listen to them both as they discussed the day.

Apparently, a schedule had been hammered out while she slept! She smiled into her cup, her eyes peeking up over at Todd. Still, as nice as ever.

She looked over at Jenny who was giving her a knowing look. "What?" she asked quietly, staring back at Jenny but feeling a blush creeping up her neck.

"Uh-huh. You know what?" Jenny whispered back. She grinned at her. "Todd, you're up for the Tongass tour today, right?"

Todd turned to them from the stove where he was pouring himself another cup of coffee. "Wouldn't miss it!" he exclaimed cheerfully.

*****

Jenny was biting her fingernails again. *If you would just relax*, she thought to herself disgustedly.

She had run upstairs after breakfast to get ready for the Tongass tour, which was, of course, where Steve worked. It was stupid of her to be uncomfortable around him, but ever since he had stopped in at Maggie's with Eileen from church, she had trouble looking him in the eyes. She constantly chided herself that it was ridiculous for her to feel this way, and she wanted him to be happy, but, well, the long and short of it was she had come to the nasty realization that day in the coffeehouse that Steve interested her as more than just a friend. Right or wrong, the feelings were there. She didn't want him sitting down with Eileen or any other girl at her table, and she most certainly did not want to ever again paste a smile on her face and wait on their table either!

With the realization, however, came the humiliation of knowing she had completely blown it with him. Never mind that it went against everything she believed in. Never mind he had not completely given himself to God yet. Never mind the countless times she had told the teens in the youth group to stay away from relationships that were outside of God to wait on God for the right person. None of that seemed to matter when you were interested enough.

She was uncomfortably aware of the fact that she was willing to compromise. *Great Christian*, she thought to herself.

She desperately missed her mom. She wanted to confide in her, to get her advice on the issue although she knew her mother would caution her. She also knew her mother would not have agreed. She had always been uncompromising with her *God walk* as she put it. What she missed most, however, was knowing with absolute certainty that her mom would have prayed about it. She believed in prayer, and she wanted to know someone was praying for her.

She was ashamed to tell Laura what she was thinking and feeling. Laura was so steadfast. She was a missionary, for goodness' sake. Laura would never compromise her beliefs for feelings; the tears threatened to come, and Jenny felt that old anger bubbling to the surface—anger that she had her parents taken so cruelly from her, anger that she was alone! Why was God so hard on her? Why did He expect so much from her?

"Jenny! C'mon! We have to go," Todd yelled from downstairs.

She hurriedly brushed at the tears and took one last look in the mirror.

"I'm coming. Two seconds!" She threw her lipstick and her brush into her backpack and moved down the stairs where Laura was eagerly waiting with Todd by the door.

Laura was holding Tyler by the hand, and he looked up at her, smiling. Jenny forgot about herself for a minute as she looked at the three of them. Todd leaned over and said something to Laura who smiled up at him in return. They look like a family. *Yes!*

CHAPTER *15*

. . . .

THEY PULLED INTO THE parking lot, and immediately, Jenny spied Steve's Jeep parked near the entrance. The butterflies started, but she ignored them and concentrated on Laura, who was exclaiming over the mountains. "It's beautiful." She breathed. "I feel God's presence so strongly," she said it with absolute sincerity, tears shining in her eyes.

They moved toward the welcome center excitedly and moved by Laura's reaction—all except Tyler, who squirmed in Todd's arms excited to be out with everyone. He kept saying, "Down, Dad."

Steve was working the desk and looked up with a smile as they came in. Jenny felt the blush creeping up her neck into her cheeks. She was sure anyone looking at her could see she was falling for him.

"Hey, Todd, Jen."

"Hey, Steve! This is Jen's friend, Laura. She's here for a visit, and we thought we would take her on the eleven o'clock tour." As Todd made the introductions, Steve came around from behind the desk to shake Laura's hand.

"Nice to meet you! Welcome. Hey, let me see if someone else can work the desk, and I will take you guys on the tour myself!"

He spoke into his walkie-talkie and received an affirmative. Jenny was frantically looking at anything but him.

The welcome center was kind of busy this time of the year, and she knew he was going out of his way to be nice to them or, at least, being nice because of Laura. She doubted that it had anything to do with her.

"It will be a few minutes before I can take you guys, but we are on!" Steve said.

"Great. That will be amazing. I'm sure you have all the inside information," Laura said.

"Um, I'm just going to run to the ladies' room," Jenny said, already hurrying away.

"Hang on, Jenny." Laura hurried after her. "I'll go with you."

They left the boys and scooted off to the ladies' room. With Laura watching her in the mirror, Jenny finally laughed and said, "What? Why are you staring at me?"

Laura gave her a sly look. "Why haven't you mentioned Steve in your letters? He is obviously of great interest to you." She gestured at the lipstick in Jenny's hand.

Embarrassed and turning red, she tried to deflect. "He started going to church a while ago. I never mentioned him?" she asked innocently.

"Not *one* time," Laura replied. She lifted her eyebrows in a stop being cute gesture and waited for Jenny to elaborate.

Jenny wrinkled her nose in distaste and confessed, "He doesn't have a relationship with the Lord." Her look dared Laura to make something of it, but Laura surprised her.

"Hmm. Well, that I'm sure that's a temporary situation." She let it drop and with a smile said, "Come on, you look great! Let's go!"

Jenny hugged her impulsively, and they went back out to the desk ready to tackle the afternoon.

Steve's enthusiasm for the Alaskan wilderness was contagious. The morning was spent with them all taking a nature hike, Tyler alternating between clinging protectively to Todd's hand when something scared him to pulling his hand away to explore. Steve discussed how each plant and animal was important in some way to the native Indian population. Steve remarked on the fact that when there was a good visibility of Mount McKinley, Alaskans say, "The mountain is out today."

The majestic mountain, which the locals call Denali, had an Athabascan name meaning, "the great one," and today was in full view and breathtaking in its grandeur. Since he was with them, he also threw in a few thoughts about God's hand in creating all of it.

Jenny watched him and reflected quietly in her heart about him. He obviously had a growing love for the Lord evidenced by the way he was not ashamed to speak about God. Maybe saying he didn't have a relationship with God was a bit judgy.

It was 70 degrees and sunny, but Jenny could tell Laura was cold. She had been on the mission field since after high school and was used to a much more tropical environment. When she saw her hugging herself and rubbing her arms to try and get warm, she nudged Todd and gave him one of her patented significant looks as she pointed at Laura.

"Hey, Laura, are you cold?" Todd asked. "I have an extra sweater." Todd came up next to her and offered her his sweater.

"I am a little." She smiled, taking it.

Jenny looked on approvingly.

Steve was pausing on the trail, waiting for them all to gather around him.

"Todd, you might want to take Tyler's hand. We are coming up to a very special place in the park," Steve spoke with a smoothness born of repeating the same thing a thousand times, but Jenny could also tell that the place was indeed special to him no matter how many times he had to repeat the same speech.

"This overhang"—he pointed to a railing overlooking a vast plain below—"gives you a view of a popular watering hole for the animals. It's a great spot for viewing the wildlife."

They crowded to the railing, and Laura gasped at the sight. Twenty-five feet below them was a great open space and a river creating a basin that was filled with turquoise water. They all *oohed* and *aahed* until all four of them were laughing.

Steve was pointing at a fox that was just coming out of the trees moving toward the water.

"What does he have in his mouth?" Jenny asked.

They all squinted, trying to make it out. Steve pulled out a pair of binoculars and took a closer look.

"It's a marmot," Steve said.

The girls cried, "Yuck!" in unison.

The fox dropped the rodent on the ground to take a drink of water and then stuffed the marmot back in his mouth and sauntered off. They stayed at the post until another group approached and then continued walking. They saw caribou, moose, and a huge Dall ram. Steve told them how lucky they had been to see so much activity on one trip.

It was after two, and they were all getting tired. Todd had picked up Tyler to carry him. They went back to the welcome center and collapsed on a bench. There was a small area for refreshments, and the adults took a much needed break from walking. Jenny volunteered to get coffee for everyone. She got up from the bench, rolling her eyes and grunting as her feet protested.

"Hey, Jenny, let me help you," Steve quickly got up as he spoke.

She smiled her thanks and moved with him up to the counter.

She felt two sets of eyes on her back and looked back for a moment. Laura was looking at Todd a small smile quirking around the corners of her mouth. He raised his eyebrow and smiled back. She hoped they were working on their own romance and not discussing hers.

"Careful, Jen." Steve put his hand on her back to direct her around a couple of tourists that had stopped to look at a map.

She had been so busy, trying to figure out what that look between Todd and Laura meant she had almost run them over.

"Sorry!" Jen moved around them embarrassed. *Ugh, could I be a bigger klutz?* She shrugged at Steve.

"My bad."

"What were you looking at?" he asked curiously.

"Oh, just checking out the chemistry between my brother and Laura!"

Steve raised an eyebrow. "Is there chemistry?"

"Seriously? You can't tell?"

"Are you sure you aren't just indulging in some wishful thinking?" Steve said, laughing.

Jen grinned back. "Well, it might be slightly premature, but I have high hopes!" Her eyes twinkled mischievously.

"Well, I'm a big believer in romance, so I will hope right along with you!" Steve replied enthusiastically.

Jenny looked at his back as he got in line for the coffee. *Wait. What? Did he just say he's a big believer in romance? Oh my.* "Laura always had a crush on my brother when we were in school, but he was older, so he didn't pay any attention to my friends. Don't tell her I told you that," Jenny said, clamping a hand over her mouth. "She would kill me if she knew I just said that."

"Your secret is safe with me, Jen," Steve said, smiling. "I won't tell her how bad you are with secrets."

"I'm not bad with secrets!" Jenny punched him lightly in the arm. "In fact, I would say I'm more like a vault! Do you know how many things people tell me, especially the teens in confidence that I never repeat?"

"No, but if you're about to tell me, then my point will be proven." Steve laughed as Jenny gave him a glare.

"Ha ha. I'm trustworthy," Jenny said, smiling.

"I know you are, Jen," Steve said suddenly serious. "You're amazing." He looked at her for a long moment.

Jenny suddenly found breathing a problem. She stared into Steve's eyes and swallowed. "I, um, oh, it's our turn." Jenny looked away, breaking the moment as Steve stepped forward to place their order. She glanced at Steve standing next to her out of the corner of her eye, and he was still watching her.

"Here ya go, Jen. Hold these two while I grab some napkins, will ya?" Steve said.

Jenny nodded, having gone mute. *Snap out of it, Milner. You are making a giant fool of yourself.* Jen shook her head clear as Steve came back with the napkins.

"Steve, thanks again for today. I, um…I had a really great time," Jen said. Her cheeks felt hot, and she looked away.

"You are very welcome. I would love to do it again some time," Steve replied. "But someone, not naming any names, told me it wasn't gonna happen," Steve continued with a teasing tone. "If that someone changes her mind, I would be thrilled."

Cheeks flaming, Jen smiled. "If that someone tells me in secret that they would enjoy doing that, I'm afraid I would not be able to repeat it. Because I'm a vault." Jenny laughed at his expression, but the conversation was halted as they met up with their group.

"Okay, everyone. Coffee is here." Jenny smiled back at Steve who was a step behind her. He quirked an eyebrow at her and mouthed, "Touché," just for her.

*****

They were sprawled on Jenny's bed late the next evening. The house was quiet. Todd had gone to bed hours ago after a hectic day at the newspaper. Jenny and Laura had shopped all morning and had lunch at a cute restaurant in town. They were exhausted but couldn't seem to stop talking.

The window was open in Jenny's room, and the crickets were busy conducting a symphony for the two girls to listen to. It was so peaceful. Laura stretched out and settled in with a contented sigh with her head propped against the headboard.

"Does Todd usually go to bed so early?" Laura asked curiously. Todd had been in bed by nine.

"That's how Todd deals with stress," Jenny replied softly. "He's always been like that. Straight to bed and things will be better in the morning," Jenny sighed.

Laura nodded and then thoughtfully looked at Jenny. "How do you deal with stress?" She was giving her the once over with a concerned eye.

"I can never eat when I'm upset. It goes right through me," Jenny admitted. She hesitated before she went on. "We've had a bit of trouble around here lately that I didn't tell you about."

Laura turned to her inquisitively and waited while Jenny gathered her thoughts.

"It's about Todd and the baby," Jenny said quietly.

Laura felt a stirring of alarm. She had grown so attached to both of them, all of them in her short time here. It was like they had an instant connection. Of course, she had been keeping up with their ups and downs, through Jenny for the last few years, so it wasn't like they were strangers. She didn't want anything to be wrong. They had all been through so much already. She waited for Jenny to go on.

"Caroline has sued for custody." Jen's words were laced with venom.

Laura didn't have to ask how she felt about Caroline.

Caroline was Todd's ex-wife, she reminded herself. Laura remembered how badly that situation had gone and how Jenny had felt flying to Todd's rescue, how angry she had been at the hurt inflicted on her brother. Jenny was fiercely protective of Todd and Tyler. Laura turned it all over in her mind.

"Can she do that?" she asked hesitantly. "I mean, she never even took care of Tyler, right? She left. What about two weeks after he was born?"

Jenny was nodding her head vigorously. "Todd tried to find her. He was even going to take her back *again* after all that." She rolled her eyes, leaving no doubt about what she thought of her brother's idea at the time. "I mean, seriously, how much is a person expected to take?"

Laura knew Jenny was expecting her to jump in and agree wholeheartedly with her, but she couldn't jump on the "I hate Caroline" bandwagon. She shrugged, trying for noncommittal.

"What?" Jenny asked sharply. "You don't agree?"

Laura pulled back defensively, hugging a pillow to her chest. "Don't be mad, Jenny."

"I'm sorry, Laura, I didn't mean to sound mad. I'm not mad. I *want* your input."

Still, Laura hesitated, then taking a deep breath, she said slowly, "It's just that sometimes, Jen, you are—she groped for the right words...so hard on people."

She saw Jen's eyes fill with tears.

"Oh, Jen, don't be upset. I'm sorry I said anything!"

Jenny shrugged. "If that's how you feel."

Her words sounded stiff and forced, and Laura knew she had offended her. "Oh, Jen, don't be like that." Laura spoke gently. "We all need correction sometime. We all need a friend to tell us when we might be a *little* wrong," She deliberately emphasized the little garnering, a small smile from Jenny.

Jenny threw her hands up in the air. "You're right, of course. Ugh. I *am* hard on people. I just hate having those light bulb moments when you see your flaws just *ugh, painfully* clear. Caroline was just so wrong to do what she did."

"I'm not saying she was right, Jen. Yes, what she did was selfish and immature. It hurt Todd, and it hurt the baby, but we don't know what she was feeling or how she feels about it now. Maybe she is trying to make amends. The point is we don't know, and you can't judge her. Jen, she's not even a Christian. How can you expect her to act like one?" She put her hand on Jenny's and squeezed it in support. "All I'm saying is don't jump to conclusions. You have to meet people where they are. How can she change? Why would she change if she doesn't see the love and forgiveness we are supposed to show as disciples of Christ?" She saw the tears sliding down Jenny's cheeks and could do nothing to stop them. It was good for her. Tears were a good thing. She scooted over to her and hugged her.

"I'm such an awful person!" Jenny cried.

"Oh, Jen, you are not. Dramatic, yes." She felt Jen stiffen. "Calm down! I'm just kidding. You are a good and godly woman who believes in doing right. You can't understand why people choose to do wrong. Everything is black and white to you. It's a good quality and a bad quality. Good because it makes you loyal and dependable and a woman of your word. Bad because you let judgment fall on people who don't or can't try as hard as you. You need to keep the good qualities and temper the judgment with compassion for people's failings."

"How, Laura? Tell me how? I don't know how to do that. Tell me how to do that!"

Laura smiled at her impatience. It was all or nothing with Jen. She was truly a unique individual. "Give it to God. Let Him change you. It's not going to be instantaneous. You have to let the changes come. You see what needs to be changed now, so the *process* will start. It just takes time." She looked at her watch, suddenly exhausted. "I need to go to bed."

"Oh, Laura. What am I going to do when you leave?"

Laura smiled as she got off the bed. "You're going to lean on your Creator and believe that He is good, and He does good for all His children."

With those words and one final hug, she went to bed.

CHAPTER *16*

. . . .

THERE WAS SO MUCH commotion in the basement at church that Laura couldn't hear herself think. She watched with amazement as people flowed in and out in ever increasing numbers carrying all manner of dishes, pots, and platters of food. The children ran back and forth, calling to each other as the adults dropped off their contributions to the picnic in the kitchen.

Laura had shied away from all the activity unsure of herself, but Jenny had only let her adjust for five minutes before she commandeered her to get the food ready to transport by covering the containers that needed it with tinfoil and plastic wrap and also to find serving spoons for the salads. That had kept her occupied for the last hour.

Laura forgot about being shy and was now trading quips with the rest of the ladies that were helping. Laura even joined in the laughter when one of the single guys from church came in carrying chicken in a bucket he had picked up in town as his contribution. He smiled sheepishly, taking the laughter and cheering from the ladies in stride but making a quick exit.

Likely, she thought, before any of the other guys found him in such an *unmanly* position! Laura liked the fact that here, women and men mixed with more equality than in the small village she was ministering too.

In that village, an unmarried man would never have thought to bring something to a church picnic. His mom or sister would have taken care of something like that.

Being an independent American woman made that part of the job difficult for her to deal with. She championed the little girls of the village and told them frequently they could dream for bigger things.

"Laura?" She heard her name and looked up at a smiling Steve Baltyn.

"Hello, Steve," she smiled shyly in return.

He was holding a box of store-bought cookies. "Where should I dump these?" he asked her.

Laura had a brilliant flash of inspiration. "Jenny is right over there. She will take those off your hands," she said it with studied casualness and watched him closely for his reaction. She was rewarded when she spied a flush creeping over his collar and the sudden flash of that indefinable *something* in his eyes that he shuttered so quickly if she had not been looking for it; she would have missed it.

"Oh, okay," he hesitated a moment more like he was about to say something but just nodded to her and smiled heading off in the direction she had sent him.

A smile played on Laura's lips as she congratulated herself on her cleverness. *You're welcome, Jenny.*

Jenny was busy organizing and packing into boxes the dishes people were handing her and laughing with the folks that were helping her. She turned around to remark to the woman behind her on the great turnout, and when she turned back to the table, Steve was standing in front of her. Her stomach flipped, but she smiled calmly enough and took the proffered cookies.

I could have been an actress. I am getting really good at pretending this guy doesn't send me over the edge. It's a good thing he can't read my mind. I would be in serious trouble.

Their eyes met, and Jenny realized suddenly that she was just staring at him and quickly looked away. Slowly the heat creeped up her neck and into her cheeks. *No, no, no. Not now.* When she blushed, the whole world could see it because of her pale skin, not to mention the fact that it could give her a headache. She swallowed, and clearing her throat, she squeaked out, "Oh, um, great. This is great. Thanks, Steve. Could you, um, excuse me?" Dropping the cookies and fleeing the table, Jen made a beeline for the table where she had left Laura.

"Hey, there, Jen." Laura smiled at her sweetly.

Jenny didn't say anything, just looked at her stupidly. "Oh, I…gosh, idiotic, feel stupid…don't know what I'm *doing*," Jenn groaned into her hands.

"Yeah, I didn't understand a word you just said. What is happening right now?" Laura was literally laughing in her face.

"Laura, it's not funny. Steve dropped off some cookies, and I just stared at him. Oh, and let's not forget turning as red as could be on top of it. Why…why is this happening to me!"

Laura shook her head in mock-sadness and handed her a box of silverware and napkins. Then she dumped the colored string in the middle of them. "No better distraction than work. Here. Help me roll up the silverware. I need to do at least fifty, more judging by this crowd, and we have less than an hour to get it all together!"

Jen picked one up and started working on automatic pilot.

"Jen?" Laura said, laughing. "This is some poor workmanship." Laura picked up the last silverware bundle Jen had wrapped. Two forks and a spoon peeked out of the knotted napkin that was already unravelling.

Jenny looked at it and shrugged. "Woops."

"I'll just go ahead and fix that." Laura slid the napkin out of Jenny's hand and covered a laugh turning back to her task. Looking up at Laura, Jenny shrugged again helplessly. "Don't worry, Laura. I got this. I promise. No more distractions!" She punctuated the promise with a fork flourish, and they both laughed.

The two of them worked side by side, and soon Jenny was forgetting about her embarrassment and laughing and talking about the picnics from years past. Recalling for Laura, the many incidents that had happened—both funny and not so funny—as in the time Todd and some other boys decided to pretend a hornet's nest was a piñata and sent two kids to the emergency because they were covered in stings.

The hour flew by, and soon they were packing up the vans that would take all the stuff for the picnic to the waterfront site the picnic had been held at since before Jenny was born. In the rush, Jenny found herself looking around for Todd. She quickly scanned the parking lot, but in the confusion of slamming doors and people calling out to each other, she figured she was missing him somehow. She shaded her eyes with her hands and scanned the thinning crowd. *Where is he? Where is Laura?* She gave a disgusted *humph!*

"They left me," she fumed. *Great. Now what am I going to do?*

She looked around to see who she could catch a ride with, but the parking lot had emptied out fast. Her eyes lighted on the red Jeep. Steve. Her stomach did a flip. *No way. There must be someone else.* Her options, however, were not looking good. *I cannot believe Laura took off without me. Had to be Todd's idea.*

The thoughts swirled around in her head in a jumble. She probably looked like an idiot standing in the lot. Her face had to be classic. *Honestly, someone should just follow me around with a video camera taping me. My life is a reality show waiting to happen.*

She rolled her eyes and braced as Steve came out of the building carrying a cooler and caught sight of her. He headed in her direction as she stood rooted to the spot. "Hey, Jen." He looked at her, smiling. "You stuck for a ride?"

"No, Steve, I just thought I would stand here and test out my theory of wishing myself somewhere." She paused. "Darn, doesn't work. I'm still standing in the parking lot."

He grinned at her sarcasm. "Cute. C'mon, I'll take you. I've got room."

Jenny was uncharacteristically quiet in the front seat as Steve drove. "Thanks," she said in a contrite tone. "I can't believe Todd and Laura left me." She blew her bangs out her eyes with an exasperated huff.

"Maybe they wanted some alone time? I thought you were pushing for a romance here?"

"Ya think?" Jenny responded hesitantly. "I can't imagine Todd being that forward, but maybe. Wadda I know? If I thought that was the case, I wouldn't be bothered at all! It's probably just a miscommunication. He must have thought I was going with someone else."

Jenny saw a strange look pass over Steve's face and swore she saw the corners of his mouth go up in a smile. He just made a noncommittal sound however and kept his eyes on the road.

Jenny relaxed as they made small talk the rest of the ride. Laughing at one of his stories, she was disappointed when they pulled up at the lakefront. The ride to the park was over much too quick, in her opinion.

Jenny wasn't sure what was going on. She and Steve had been at the picnic for over an hour, and still, no sign of Todd or Laura or even the baby. Instead, Steve had guided her to a spot under a tree near everyone but still slightly private and had spread down a blanket and told her to sit. She had done so willingly, although she made a face at him just to keep him from thinking she was going to be bossed around all the time.

She didn't want him to know how much it thrilled her that he was bossing her around. She thought it was cute. Nor was she inclined to insist that they look for her brother or Laura. She hated to admit it to herself, but she would be more than content to sit with Steve, just the two of them under that tree all day, every day. She couldn't figure out however why he seemed so content to hang out with *her*. She figured he would be looking around for his *friend—Eileen*. Yuck, even when she said her name in her head, she said it with a hateful little tone. For someone who had never been the jealous type, she had to admit she was jealous this time. She was ashamed of herself for feeling that way, but for the life of her, she couldn't seem to stop doing it.

Eileen sure wasn't at fault and neither was Steve, if she was in a generous mood. She was just going to have to keep putting the damper on those feelings when they came up.

That's all I'd need is for someone to catch me rolling my eyes at the two of them when they're having an innocent conversation. Real mature.

This falling for someone was not as simple as people said. The roller-coaster ride of emotions she was feeling frankly left her exhausted. The more she tried not to think of him, the more he was in her thoughts.

She saw him approaching, carrying two heaping plates of food. She cocked her head and looked at him as he struggled to balance the plates and not drop anything.

He is too good to be true, she thought with a sigh. *How am I supposed to keep my feelings in check when he acts like this? He's just being nice*, she tried to convince herself. *He probably does this with every girl. I'm going to wind up looking like a goof if I let on I'm affected by it. I'm sure how I feel about him is written all over my face.*

Steve sat down next to her grinning. He deposited one of the plates into her lap, and as she reached for it, their hands touched. He didn't move his hand right away, and Jenny stared at it frozen for a moment unable to blink. She gulped and looked up into his eyes with a flush creeping up her neck. He stared into her eyes with a soft little smile playing about his lips, and she was lost. She couldn't have said a word if her life depended on it. Steve leaned toward her, and Jenny's eyes opened wider in surprise.

Oh my god, he's going to kiss me, she thought, and at that moment, she wanted nothing more than for that to happen.

She wanted him to kiss her. Despite the fact that they weren't dating, despite the fact he wasn't a Christian, despite the fact that they were in full view of practically the entire church and would probably cause a scandal, she wanted him to kiss her. Instead, he hesitated and reached out his hand to tuck a piece of her wayward hair back behind her ear.

She was disappointed, yes, but another part of her thrilled at that touch. It seemed so, so intimate she finally decided. Her hands were a little shaky as she situated the plate in her lap. "Thanks," she said softly, gesturing to the food.

"No problem, Ma'am." He affected an acute Southern drawl. "I'm here to be of service to y'all." He doffed his imaginary hat at her and succeeded in spilling his plate. "Ugh!" he exclaimed as he tried to salvage his food.

Jenny collapsed, laughing. She laid on her own best Southern drawl. "Why, sir? Please don't you worry about that. Why I have enough here to share? You've been so kind and all." She batted her eyelashes at him, and he grinned ear to ear.

"You crack me up, Jenny. That's one of the things I like about you."

She couldn't resist. "One of the things?" she asked him with a voice full of innocence.

"Yes, one of things, one of the many things, if you must know. And if you think you're getting any more compliments out of me, well, you'll just have to wait. One or two more might slip out at some point," he finished, grinning wickedly at her.

There goes another blush, she thought her face warming. *Grief.*

She took the opportunity to hide behind her hair for a minute and compose herself while Steve dove into what was left on his plate. She was enjoying being with him. A lot. She could only hope he was feeling the same. *He must be feeling it too*, she thought, *or why would we be sitting here by ourselves?*

She hoped he didn't want to be just friends. She didn't think she could do that. Every time he was around, she felt electrified. She caught her errant thoughts and again felt the conviction of the Holy Spirit nudging her. She needed to be careful about these feelings. Feelings were deceptive. Feelings weren't facts. Feelings could lead you far from the path God had for you. She nodded to herself. She was going to have to keep this above board and depend on the Lord for guidance and self-control.

She was lost in her thoughts when she looked up and realized Steve was looking at her. He had a funny half smile on his face. *Adorable*, she sighed to herself.

"What?" she asked him.

He looked at her shrewdly. "What would you do if I asked you out? Hypothetically?"

She didn't answer right away because she knew she was on dangerous ground. In her mind, she thought, *I'd say yes so fast it would make your head spin.* Out loud she responded airily, "Hypothetical, right?"

He quickly nodded, watching her.

She tilted her head like she was giving it great thought. "Well," she paused, "I would say no." *He looked a little crushed,* she thought. *Hooray!* "But," she continued, "I would have to put a disclaimer on that." She looked at him all innocence.

"What do you mean a disclaimer?"

"Well, I would have to add that persistence pays."

He smiled at her. "Persistence, ay? So how many times, hypothetically, would I have to ask you out to qualify as persistence? Before I could expect that yes?"

She looked at him and said with mock seriousness, "Twice."

"*Twice!*" He choked out incredulously. "Twice is persistent to you?"

"I'm sorry," she said tartly. "Is that a complaint?"

"No complaints here. I prefer your definition of persistence to the one I had previously held!"

They both collapsed, laughing.

Jenny wiped the tears from her eyes, thinking about how much she enjoyed going back and forth with him kidding when she caught him staring again.

"What now?" she asked, smiling.

Steve held her gaze.

Man, he has pretty eyes, she thought out of nowhere.

"Jen? Would you go out with me?"

Her smile twitched. "No."

She held his gaze challenging him. She was enjoying this way too much.

"*Jen*, please, would you go out with me?"

There it was two times on the table.

Jen narrowed her eyes, still not breaking from his gaze. She shook her head no.

"Hey," he complained, "that's not fair. You said persistence pays."

She stuck her tongue out at him, keeping the mood light. "*You* said it was hypothetical." She had him there.

"We are going to revisit this at a later date."

She smiled at him on top of the world. "I should hope so," she answered demurely.

He reached out and touched her cheek, leaving his hand there. The smile left her face as she watched him, her heart pounding loudly.

"You are something else, Jen," he spoke softly and then suddenly moved his hand away. With a groan, he stood up and then reached down and offered a hand to help her up. She was speechless; sure that if she spoke at all, she would be completely incoherent.

"C'mon, Jen, let's go find your brother before I do something I'll regret."

She followed after him; her hand firmly held in his hand without saying a word.

The debate in her mind lasted through the next ten minutes of looking over the grounds to find Laura and her brother. The usual stuff. Should she be with him at all? Was the Lord in this? Would God put someone in her life she was so attracted to for nothing? Was it even God? Maybe Satan had placed a snare for her to get caught in, and she was walking right into the trap.

She finally started an honest prayer. One that wasn't just give me what I want, Lord. One she prayed from her heart. *Lord, if You're in this, please make a way. Show him You are real and waiting for him to trust You, but, God, if this isn't You, if this is the enemy trying to make me fall, then please show me.*

Take the feelings away. Slam the door shut on this before it gets harder than it is already. Give me wisdom, Lord. I need You. Above all, help me to please You.

Her amen was said quietly, and she immediately felt the presence of God.

She smiled at Steve and slipped her hand out of his. If he was upset, he didn't show it.

They continued on until she spied Todd throwing a Frisbee to Laura while Tyler ran around picking it up when it fell. She smiled at them gladly they were getting along so well because Laura felt like a sister.

She looked up at Steve, and before he knew what she was up to, she took off running, yelling, "Race ya!" As she sped toward Laura, she could hear him laughing behind her and shouting, "No fair. Cheater!"

Steve easily overtook her even with the lead she had. Considering his legs were about twice as long as hers, she wasn't surprised. As he sped past her, he taunted her, "C'mon, cheater! Not so cocky now, huh!"

She laughed.

They both arrived breathless and collapsed on the grass next to Todd and Laura. Tyler was thrilled to see her and as always took the opportunity to throw himself on her. She wrestled him to the ground, tickling him. All she could think was *What a perfect day.*

*****

She drove home with her brother and Laura after thanking Steve for the offer but declining a ride home. She smiled at the disappointment; she had seen lurking in his eyes when she took a pass. It had been the most perfect day that Jen could ever remember having. She felt like all her body was tingling. She felt completely alive. She didn't want to ruin it, so she figured ending it on a high note was a safe bet. She would never tell him what an effort it was to take a pass. Of course, she wanted to ride home with him. She just knew what she wanted was conflicting with how she was supposed to behave.

She wandered down to the kitchen after putting on her pajamas and put on the teakettle. She settled in a chair next to Laura who had the same idea. They smiled at each other.

"It was a perfect day, don't you think?" Jenny spoke softly.

"Mmm," Laura agreed with a nod.

"Laura, do you think I'm doing anything wrong?" she spoke hesitantly, anxious and not sure if she even wanted an answer.

Laura took her time responding and finally said very softly, "I think you know. I think you know what you have to do." Laura's voice was gentle but firm as she continued, "Jenny, if your mom were here, I believe she would say the same thing to you that I am going to say. Be his friend, and nothing more until he commits to the Lord. If you think you can't do that, be honest with yourself and put some distance between the two of you. You have to guard your heart since you don't know if this can go anywhere. You can't just say, 'Here's the man I want!' You must be able to say, 'Here is a man I can follow,' until he can lead you closer to the One who is above all things. He cannot be the man you need."

Impulsively, Jen reached over and hugged her. There were tears forming in her eyes but a new determination in her jaw. "I needed to hear that. It confirms everything the Lord has been trying to tell me. Thanks for being honest."

Laura looked pained. "*Umm*, Jen, I have a little confession to make, which in light of what I just said to you is gonna sound bad."

"What is it?" Jenny asked, surprised.

"I may have participated in a plan today to kinda stick you with Steve on purpose. Todd and I thought, well, it seemed like the right thing to do at the time. We left you on purpose."

"*Are you serious!* Wait, whose idea was this? Todd's?"

Laura looked at her lips pursed together. "Steve's."

Jenny rocked back in her seat blown away by the turn of events. "That punk. I can't believe he set me up!" Far from upset, Jenny started laughing. "And I can't believe you goofs went along with him!"

"Well, like I said, it seemed like a good idea at the time." Laura smiled at her mischievously, "So just to be clear, you're not mad?"

Jenny grinned, "I'm not mad. I feel so much better. I thought I was making a complete fool out of myself today. I'm glad you told me!"

Laura pretended to wipe sweat from her brow. "Whew! I didn't want you to think I was a big hypocrite. Steve is a nice guy. I hope it works out. I just don't want you to get ahead of yourself, and I sure didn't help today."

"It's fine, Laur. I feel a real peace about this. I think we are going to be fine."

CHAPTER 17

LAURA WAS PACKING. EVERYONE was moping around the house, trying to tiptoe around the fact that she was leaving. Two weeks had flown by! She had become part of the family from the first day. A perfect fit. The reality that it was all about to change weighed heavy on each one of them.

Todd hasn't said two words all morning, Jenny thought startled. She had been so miserable herself she hadn't realized how upset he was.

Laura was the only one completely calm. She was the picture of tranquility. Jenny eyed her from her spot on the bed as she watched her fold her clothes into her suitcase. *Miserable quality,* she thought to herself. *Why can't she get upset like a normal person?* She stared hard at her. Laura must have felt her eyes boring into her because she suddenly looked up and with a quizzical look and said, "What is it? Is something wrong?"

Jenny let out a very unladylike snort. "How is it possible," she began, "that you are so completely fine today? It's driving me insane! I can't believe you're leaving. I don't want you to go!" That last bit came out on the beginning of a sob, and she knew she was going to start crying again.

Laura rushed to the bed and enveloped her in a big hug. "Oh, Jenny, I will miss you! Your dramatic flare, your big heart! It doesn't mean that I'm not sad to go. I am just leaning on the arms of Jesus, and He is giving me *His* sweet peace in this situation exactly because *it is* too hard for me! I have to believe that His plan is best. I can't stay right now, but who knows what the future holds?" She straightened up from the bed and smiled. "C'mon, make my last day here special. Let's not ruin it with tears, okay?"

"Okay," Jenny said less enthusiastically. Suddenly, with a gleam in her eye, she uttered another dramatic sigh and slyly added, "I can't guarantee, however." She paused, looking very sad. "I can't guarantee," she continued, "the same thing for my brother. He seems to be taking this worse than I am." She was rewarded by Laura blushing beet red.

"Oh, Jenny," she said, smiling into her suitcase.

They looked up and met each other's eyes and cracked up.

CHAPTER *18*

TODD WAS QUIET. HE and Jenny had dropped Laura off at the airport early that afternoon, and he was desperately trying to distract himself at work. The hole he felt at her leaving was threatening to overtake his senses. He was usually a practical man.

He was divorced, he reminded himself.

True, it wasn't his fault or his desire to be divorced, but the bottom line was he was. He didn't think Laura would be interested in someone with an ex-wife. She could do better. He was also in the midst of a custody battle. Okay, maybe not a battle but an uncomfortable situation.

He ran his hands through his hair and gave his head a good shake to clear the cobwebs. *That's a lot of baggage for someone to deal with*, he thought. He stood up from his desk and slapped his hand down. *Enough!* He noted that he had startled his assistant who was looking at him like he was crazy. "Sorry. I was just thinking about something," he explained lamely, sitting back down in his chair.

He had been yelling at himself quite a bit lately. *Probably, time to talk to the Pastor about it*, he allowed himself. *He can help me work through these feelings.*

He hated to admit they even existed. He felt like it was a weakness he needed to squash. How could he fault his sister for her romantic feelings for Steve when his own were just as out of control?

He picked up his phone on the first ring. "Hello, this is Todd." Todd listened as his lawyer spoke. He had never minded Mondays before. In fact, he was usually energized from Sunday and never one of those people who lamented, "I hate Mondays." This Monday, however, was the worst!

He listened intently, nodding occasionally in agreement and murmuring, "Yes, I understand." He could see the members of his staff trying to keep their noses buried in their work with their eyes firmly on their laptops, giving him as much privacy as a small-time paper housed in one room allowed.

His entire staff was aware of what was going on in his personal life. Every one of them was unequivocally on his side.

Todd hung up the phone and looked around at his staff *not* looking at him and allowed himself a tight smile. As a group as well as individually, they had offered themselves as friends, coworkers, and character witnesses to aid him. He could not believe how God had blessed him. He was not a bit sorry he had moved from Seattle and taken this job. What Satan had meant for evil God had turned to good. He was so aware of the Lord's hand on his life now that he still shook his head in wonder that he couldn't see it before.

Well, no sense looking back. He fought to keep his nerves at bay.

Larry wanted him in his office tomorrow at ten o'clock to prep him, *whatever that meant.* He needed to stay focused and calm, needed to trust that God was with him even in this new challenge. He knew that somewhere deep down, there was simmering anger just below the surface toward Caroline that he didn't dare dwell on. If he allowed himself the luxury of *how dare she*, he was doomed. He was afraid if he let himself feel that for even one moment, he couldn't be sure he wouldn't throttle her if he got the chance.

CHAPTER *19*

. . . .

STEVE HEARD THE CRACKLE of the radio and excused himself from the tourists he had been speaking with and moved back behind the counter.

"Tower to base, tower to base, this is Karen. Anyone, copy."

Steve clicked the button on his two-way radio and responded, "Tower, this is Steve at base. What can I do for you, Karen?"

Karen replied in a calm monotone voice trained not to be alarmed easily, "Steve, I need you to go secure. Repeat, I need you to go secure."

Steve instantly turned serious. To go secure meant to get to the back office and get on the radio away from the tourists. That meant trouble: Someone was hurt; an animal had become dangerous; or worst-case scenario, fire.

"Copy that, tower. I am going secure, repeat, going secure."

Steve hurried down the hall to the office, closing the door quickly behind him and gesturing for one of the other rangers who was on the phone to get off and listen in.

"What's up?" Mark asked. Mark was a ten-year veteran of the park rangers. As a former army ranger, he was adept at solving problems. He rubbed the stubble of his beard as his brown eyes bright with intelligence fixed on Steve's. "What's the trouble?"

Steve gestured to the radio. "Tower 10. Karen is in the cab this morning and said she needed me to go secure."

Mark quickly went to the radio and stood behind Steve, who was already hailing Karen. "Tower 10, this is base. Tower 10, this is base. We are secure. Repeat, we are secure. Go ahead, Karen. Mark is here with me."

Karen dropped the formality and said simply the words every ranger hates to hear, "Boys, we have a new fire."

Mark sprang into action. He raced to the desk and grabbed a pad of paper and pen.

Steve spoke into the radio deadly calm and grateful for the protocols in place to help them calmly gather information in emergencies. First, he needed confirmation. "Okay, tower, whadya got? Can you confirm the new fire? Repeat, can you confirm new fire?"

No hesitation, Karen came right back. "That is a positive command. I confirmed via the Osborne. New fire. Coordinates: Alpha, Charlie, Ten, Visual, and Osborne confirmation." There was a pause before they heard, "This could be a big one, guys."

Mark opened the door of the office and pulled a startled volunteer into the room by the arm who had been heading down the hallway. "Get the chief up here right now," he barked, scaring the kid into a dead run. Mark raced back to the desk, pulling out the drawers one after another, muttering, "Where are those things?"

Finally, finding the binoculars he was looking for, he headed for the door. "Steve, stay on with Karen at the tower. I'm heading to the overlook to see if I can spot it. Chief should be here any minute. Tell him we'll know more in five minutes."

Steve nodded and turned back to the radio. "Tower, what's your situation? How close are you to the flash point?"

"Base, I am looking at spot fire Grid, Baker, Romeo, Foxtrot, 214. Grid, Baker, Romeo, Foxtrot, 214. I am in good watch position."

Steve shook his head. That girl was one of the best, but she liked danger a little too much for him. She was never afraid of anything, and that was one dangerous trait if you asked him.

Thank God, Jenny is more practical, he thought.

He was always thinking about her at the strangest times. She seemed to creep into all the little nooks and crannies of his life. He would be doing the dishes and suddenly remember something funny she said and find himself smiling or walking to get his coffee and thinking about how much she liked coffee and wondering what she was doing right at that moment and wishing he could bring her some coffee himself. For the first time in his life, he was thinking of forever.

Forever had never before had a name attached to it, but it did now. In fact, two names—two names that seemed linked somehow: Jesus and Jenny. Jesus who was becoming an inescapable factor in his life as pressing and real as Jenny. He couldn't seem to find a way to move from the *but* to the *faith* that Pastor kept talking about.

He pushed a hand through his hair impatiently. He didn't like being undecided. It wasn't his nature, and yet that was precisely where he found himself.

His thoughts became the frustrating tangle they had been for months, and he abruptly stopped himself. "No time for this, Steve," he muttered to himself. "Get the job done. Karen, how's it looking out there?" Steve snapped into the mike, drawing a surprised look from Mark who had just come in on the heels of the chief.

"It's getting fairly windy up here, guys. I can see flames clearly coming out of the south at the top of the tree line," she didn't have to say more than that. If the fire was claiming the tree canopies, it was burning hotter and faster than anyone expected. That meant flames that could reach three hundred feet into the air and cause major damage.

Steve raised his eyebrow at the chief and motioned for him to take over.

"No, no, Steve, go ahead." He nodded at Steve to continue.

"Karen, be prepared to evacuate that tower. Copy?" Steve said.

"Copy that, Steve. I will let you know. Tower out."

Steve clicked off and met the chief's eyes and then Mark's. It was going to be a long night.

CHAPTER 20

. . . .

TODD SPED DOWN THE road as fast as he could safely. "Please let me get there first," he prayed. "Please, Lord, let me be the one to tell her."

He couldn't believe this day. It was the most awful never-ending Monday he had ever had. It seemed like a thousand years since Laura had left instead of just that afternoon.

He pulled into the driveway and jumped out of the car, sprinting for the front door. This was turning out to be a really, really bad day. First, Laura, then Larry calling him to set up a date to talk about court which was scheduled in two weeks. Now a fire that was sounding bad right in their backyard. He was beginning to understand that phrase, "When it rains, it pours."

"Jen," he yelled, "where are you?" He had smelled the smoke as soon as he left town and turned toward the house. He couldn't see flames yet, but he knew they weren't far off.

He was grateful Steve had thought to call him right away. He figured it wasn't just because he was giving him the news story, but he wanted to make sure Jen was going to be okay. If the call for evacuation didn't come today and the winds kept up, he figured by tomorrow at the latest the sheriff's patrols would be sounding the alarm. Once the sirens went off, they would only have a few hours to get out safely.

"Jen," he called again louder, trying not to sound frantic.

"I'm up here." He heard her respond. She started down the stairs toward him. "I wanted to get a load of laundry done while Tyler was taking his nap. I let everything go while Laura was here and—" She trailed off as she saw the look on his face. "What's wrong!" Her hands began to tug at her shirt which she only did when she was nervous or excited. Fear coursed through her—the kind of fear that only someone who had known the pain and tragedy she had already experienced would understand, the fear that could be controlled but never completely went away.

Todd saw the fear began to build in her and quickly went to her, drawing her down to sit next to him on the step. "Forest fire," he said quietly, trying to reassure her with a steady look.

"How big?" she asked.

"Big," Todd said quietly. He didn't add any details. He didn't have a lot of details at that point. He got up and started toward the kitchen with Jen trailing behind him. "I've already been notified by the rangers that a command post is being established in town at the rec center. They think this may be one they call a hotshot crew in for."

Jenny gasped. "Really? I can't remember the last time that happened." She looked up at her brother, a vulnerable look in her eyes. "Steve?" she asked him.

Todd hesitated. Steve was trained to participate. All the rangers were. If the hotshots were taking point, they were going to need all the men they had digging trenches in the staging area. Even though it was a safe distance behind the fire, all kinds of things could go wrong.

"I don't know, Jen." He felt completely helpless. He wanted to erase that look in her eyes.

"He's the one that took the call, and he called me right after. I don't know what else he's doing. The minute I hear anything, I'll let you know. I need you to be ready to go, Jen. Just in case it comes to that. If they call for an evacuation, I'll come back for you and Tyler, and you need to be ready to go."

He knew he sounded like his dad. It pained him to think of his parents just then. It would be so much easier to have shared the burden of this moment with them. They had such innate strength. He wanted to be strong for Jen and Tyler.

"I'm sorry, Jen, I have to go. I have to get back to the paper. You'll be ready?"

She nodded her head obediently.

He hated to leave her with all the uncertainty. He hated to leave Tyler, but he needed to make sure the reports went out. He could help get information out quickly and effectively. That could help save lives.

"It's okay, Todd. Go, do what you need to. I'll be ready. I'll take care of Ty. Just call me, okay, if you hear anything?"

He nodded. "I will, Jen. I promise. I'll call as soon as I know anything. Pray, okay, Jen? For everyone."

"I will, you know, I will." Jenny hugged him, and he hugged her tight for a few seconds.

"Okay. I have to go."

Todd took off as fast as he could and headed straight for the command post. He knew that's where all the information would be.

He was waved off the road by a cop he didn't know. Another sign that this fire was big. Obviously, people were being called in from the surrounding areas. He showed his press badge and was directed to a clearing next to the recreation center which stood alone at the end of Main Street.

Todd spotted Chief Louder surrounded by people at a table in the center of the gym. *Smart*, he thought. It was the biggest space available for miles. The town used it for everything from basketball to dances to town meetings. He made his way through the people milling around to hear what was going on.

The chief was writing on a blackboard. It looked old and had probably been stashed somewhere in the basement. *He is a commanding presence*, Todd thought not for the first time. Six feet two with bright red hair, he had a booming voice and booming fist to match.

They said fires extinguished themselves when he was near. He struck the chalk against the blackboard like it was an opponent to be bested practically causing sparks. He had everyone's undivided attention.

Chief Louder pointed at an area on the map laid out on the table. Todd craned his neck to see.

"Here's the anchor point," he boomed. "I want to drop the first team of firefighters here and here. They can start the trench work while I get the C-130 in the air. The spray zone is here and here," he continued, sending chalk dust into the air. "That will give us time to get this area evacuated."

Todd was relieved to see it was an area opposite of the house.

The chief paused and looked at the group around him. "I'm not going to sugarcoat this, people. We have a very serious situation here. We have low humidity, high temps, and strong winds. We have erratic gusts of up to 50 mph."

The men looked grave. Todd wasn't sure exactly what all of that meant, but it didn't sound good.

"We are starting out on a red flag warning," Chief Louder stressed out, and Todd knew this day was going long.

He grabbed the coat of a fireman standing next to him. "What's a red flag warning?" he asked curiously.

The fireman replied, "Extreme danger. This is only the second I've ever seen."

Todd blinked. He thanked him for the information and tried to signal to the chief that he wanted to speak with him. Chief Louder saw him and motioned for him to wait.

Todd pulled out his phone and called his lawyer. He explained the situation and said he would have to reschedule. Larry assured him it was fine. He ended the call quickly as the chief headed his way.

CHAPTER *21*

· ·

JEN HAD SETTLED INTO a state of waiting. She had gotten up
to a yellow sun glowing in a brown sky. The smoke had settled over everything as a constant reminder that just over the
ridge, something huge was going on.

The town had been put on standby for evacuation, giving her way too much time to worry. Like most of her neighbors, she had made frequent trips to the community center
and then to the high school where people were gathering to
exchange the latest news.

The high school had become a shelter of sorts for towns
in the outlying areas that had already been evacuated. Driving
was becoming dangerous as ash and soot began to blow across
the roads like dirty snow. It was a surreal experience.

She couldn't believe it was the middle of July. She found
herself spending hours watching the news crawl by on the
television even though it gave out the same information she
already had from her friends or from Todd who usually had
it right from the firemen. She also had to work because the
coffee shop was crowded with reporters and the curious. She
was grateful for the diversion.

Todd had tacked up a Tongass National Forest map on
the wall. Each time a piece of information became available,
a neighborhood evacuated, a fire map released, and Todd
would mark it on the map. They watched the progression of

the fire as it consumed more and more acres. They grieved the places that were special to them—trails they had hiked with their parents, places they had gone too with friends when they were in school. Those places would be changed forever.

The bright yellow shirts of the firemen were familiar to everyone in town. People greeted them in the grocery stores and spoke words of encouragement. Maggie told her and Dawn that all fire personnel were to have their coffee first and free. She said it was the least she could do to help them out.

As the days went by, Jen thought about Steve and prayed constantly that the Lord would protect him. Todd didn't have much news about him other than to say he was definitely working in the fire. She had not heard from him personally at all. He probably didn't want to take the time to call. It wouldn't have helped anyway. It would just remind her of the danger he was in.

Jen looked up to see Todd reporting from the community center. The newspaper owner had recently asked Todd to do live broadcasts about the fires in addition to the hard copy and web pages of the news. She turned up the volume on the television.

The army has joined the battle against the newly named Rolling Ridge fire—named after the first ridge the fire crested on Monday night. The army is hoping to hold back the flames that have advanced to the back doors of Ketchikan. We saw early this morning large pieces of earthmoving equipment, making their way out of Fort Kellogg and headed up Tongass Road on the way to one of the last trenches dug by the elite hotshot crew out of North Dakota. US Forest Service spokesman, Dan Hanrahan, said earlier today that the fire was expected to move eastward during the day, and that weather was always a major factor when fighting fires. The National Interagency Fire Center, the Idaho-based national control center for wildfire fighting, predicts a high of 80 degrees and winds blowing between 20 and 30 mph. The firefighters unfortunately can expect little help from Mother Nature. This is Todd Milner for the Ketchikan News Channel 12.

The weather gave the fire a huge jolt by that evening. Jen stood outside her front door with Tyler on her hip and could see tall dark columns of thick smoke churning in the hazy red sky. She could see flames leaping up on the nearby hillsides, the winds pushing the blaze east.

It was now less than eight miles north of their town. She shook her head. She was packed and ready to go the minute Todd came or she heard the siren go off.

CHAPTER 22

THURSDAY MORNING, CAROLINE SAT at the airport bar, waiting for her flight. She was going to fly into Anchorage and drive down to Todd's. She was sick of talking to her lawyer, sick of secondhand information, and sick of Todd. He was like cancer. He just kept eating at her no matter how hard she tried to forget him.

Nothing had worked, not burying herself in work, in partying, or dating other people. No matter how long it had been, he was always there.

The accusations hung over her head. She missed who he was before he went all *God* crazy.

As she tossed back her third drink in less than an hour, she fumed about how unfair it all was. She went over and over in her head how she had wound up at this place in her life, and it always came back to Todd. He was the problem. He had ruined everything with his ridiculous *God* stuff. He had ruined their marriage, ruined their lives, ruined her life.

Her eyes filled with tears, and she impatiently swiped at them with the back of her hand. Nothing had turned out the way she planned since she had left him, but what choice had he given her?

She didn't know why she was even getting on this stupid plane. Todd probably wouldn't even talk to her at this point. Her lawyer had absolutely forbidden her to contact Todd.

She just had to try talking to him; she didn't have anything left.

"Flight 343 to Anchorage is now boarding at Gate F."

Caroline looked up at the announcement and rose unsteadily to her feet. She collected her carry on and left the table heading toward the gates. She didn't have a plan really; she just figured if she could talk to Todd face to face, he could fix this, fix her.

Surprised by the admission even as it flitted across her consciousness, she clamped down on the thought. She needed a drink. A drink would make her feel better. At least, for a little while.

*****

She hadn't meant to stop on the drive into town, but the thought of seeing Todd again had brought on a panic attack. She thought she was having a heart attack and had pulled over to catch her breath. She figured a drink would calm her down, help to settle her.

She had pulled into the roadside bar an hour outside of Ketchikan. If she remembered correctly, she and Todd had been here a couple of times way back when. Nostalgia made her weepy. She had been sitting at the bar for hours.

The bartender had flipped the television on and was engrossed in the story. She looked up blearily at the newscaster. He was talking about a fire—a big fire from the sound of it. Slowly it started to sink in. Todd's town was being mentioned as the next town to be evacuated.

"Damn," she mumbled. Nothing went her way. She better get going before there was no one there to talk to.

His sister had never liked her. *Stupid Holy Roller*, but she would never turn her away. *She has to be nice to her whether she wanted to or not. Isn't that in some Christian code-book somewhere?*

Her thoughts were scattered all over, and she was having a hard time focusing. What had she been thinking about? *Oh yeah, Todd's sister, Jen. She is probably the one keeping the baby from her, not Todd. Todd is just being a nice guy as usual. Jen had gone off the deep end before when their parents got killed. He is probably doing this for her. He doesn't know she is ready to be a mom now. She could do it now. She just hadn't been ready before.*

She got up from the chair and, in the process, spilled her purse out on the floor. She saw the bartender looking at her. *Busybody needs to mind his own business,* she seethed, waving him off. She waved him off.

She was fine. She was used to taking care of herself. She didn't need his help or anyone's for that matter. She was just tired. Was it a crime to be tired now? Her limbs felt heavy, and she forced herself to get moving. It was getting late, wasn't it?

Oops. She stumbled over the threshold. "They should get that fixed," she mumbled.

She squinted into the parking lot. She couldn't remember what kind of car she had rented. There were just a few in the parking lot, so she headed for the one that looked familiar. She tried the key in the lock. *There. Mission accomplished,* she thought, pleased with herself. She got behind the wheel and started the car. She would just take this one step at a time. *No need to be upset,* she repeated to herself as she headed onto the road.

I'm so tired. Her eyes kept closing before she forced them open again. She watched gray snowflakes fall on the windshield.

So odd, she thought. She couldn't figure out why it seemed to be snowing in the middle of the summer. *I'll just close my eyes for a second.*

*****

The blaring horn jolted Caroline awake. Her head whipped up to see lights coming at her head on. She jerked the wheel to the right, sending her skidding toward the edge of the road.

Caroline shrieked in horror as the car slammed into the embankment and burst into flames.

"Hold on!" Richard yelled. He was trying to tap the brakes and control the skid the fire truck had been thrown into. "They came right at us!" he said shakily to his partner. Recovering his composure, he yelled, "Let's go, guys. They need help!"

The guys riding in the cab were already grabbing gear and scrambling out of the fire truck heading back to the spot the car had landed. It didn't look good for whoever it was.

*****

Todd got the call from one of his reporters at the office covering the desk. Since he was the closest, he headed toward the crash himself. He was exhausted. The last four days had been absolutely grueling. He wiped the grit from his eyes and sent up a quick prayer for the victim as well as the firemen who were trying to help.

The information he had was sketchy. Either a drunk driver or someone asleep at the wheel had crossed over the lane and caused the accident. The crash sounded bad, possibly fatal. He shook his head. Boy, it sure did seem like it was one thing after another lately.

He thought for a moment about Laura. He had felt so calm when she was around. He knew nothing could come from it. It just irked him that his life seemed to be one crisis after another and completely out of his control.

That was his constant complaint to God. He had such hopes and dreams, things he wanted to see happen, and he couldn't see that any of that was in his future. He wanted to trust God, but that was a phrase he was sure people who had everything they wanted tossed around. Not guys like him— single with a small child, no wife, a custody battle, a fire jeopardizing his home, loneliness.

He was nearing the scene of the crash. There was very little traffic because of the fire, but the few cars that were out on the road were slowing down or stopped. He pulled over a few feet away from the fire truck and hiked up to the police officer directing traffic. Todd looked up the twenty feet or so toward the crash. It looked like they were trying to get the door off the car with the jaws of life.

Todd nodded politely at the officer and showed him his press badge. The officer nodded, acknowledging him as he waved someone around the wreckage.

"Can you tell me anything yet?" Todd asked with his pencil and notepad ready.

The officer shook his head. "Don't have much information. They haven't been able to get the victim out. It's a woman, maybe early thirties. It looks like she was alone. The fire truck says she was driving on the wrong side of the road drunk or asleep most likely. They saw her coming and laid on the horn. Must have startled her because she swung right and went right into the embankment. Looks bad."

He shook his head like he had seen it all before but would never get used to it. "Thanks," Todd said and moved off, trying to get closer to the wreck without getting in anyone's way.

He took up a position near the fire truck that had been involved taking down the engine number and getting a call into the office for any and all information on that engine house for background filler for the story. He found himself wishing desperately for a cup of coffee. Commotion from the wreck had him hanging up the phone with a hurried "I'll call ya back."

The firemen were all shouting orders as the door of the vehicle came off. The paramedics rushed in. Todd was craning his neck trying to see.

CHAPTER 23

STEVE WOKE UP DISORIENTED at 6:30 a.m. after a night of tossing and turning. He was due back at base camp at 0800. The jumpers and pilots were split between two sites, the old Alaska base on airport way and the newer facility at the T-hangar at Fort Wainwright.

Todd was at Fort Wainwright. The base manager, Dennis, had issued orders last night after conferring with the fire behavior analyst, the chief, and the bureau of land management.

The rangers had spent a few hours with the hotshot's the night before going over PLFs (parachute landing falls). Steve was glad for the practice. They also had a refresher course in rappelling which came in handy if you happened to *tree up* as the smoke jumpers called it. That was a nice way of saying some schmuck landed in a tree.

The rookies looked as nervous as they felt, and everyone was feeling the pressure. This was Steve's home turf, however. It was personal for him. His home was here. His friends were here. His life was here.

He was glad he had kept up his discipline of running and lifting. He made a mental note to make sure the rookies had plenty of water in case they ran into trouble. Fire jumpers tended to be self-sufficient as a unit—everyone lending his or her particular skills and qualifications. The minute the spotter yells, "On final," they had to be totally focused and ready to go.

Steve jumped with an old friend of his in a two-man stick formation—two men at a time out of the plane. Ryan Louder was a bit of a show-off, but he was fun loving and good at what he did. Steve trusted him to have his back.

The foreman was Kevin Leato. Steve knew him by reputation as one of the best. He sized up the situation, made the decisions, yelled out the orders, picked up the trails, and set the pace. He was the man in charge of their safety.

The second in command was Mike Wojo. He was bringing up the rear. He was making sure no one got lost or headed off the trail. He repeated the orders and made sure they were understood. He also made sure the crew was acting as a team.

When they hit the fire, Kevin decided the plan of attack, and Mike encouraged or yelled at the team depending on what was needed to get everyone working at peak performance. They had worked well into the night and were back this morning to do it all again. He shook himself awake and hurried to base.

*****

Todd was sure he was dreaming, having a nightmare. He was shaking his head in disbelief, struggling to see. He headed toward the car in slow motion. The paramedics were bent over her working on her.

Yelling. He was yelling, "Caroline!" A fireman grabbed him by the arm, but Todd shook him off violently, propelling himself forward. "Let me go. I know her. Caroline!"

The paramedic was working over her, and someone was talking to him. All he could see was Caroline's face covered in blood. *God, there is so much blood. What is she doing here?*

The ambulance was here, but they weren't doing anything.

"Help her," he whispered. "Please, God, help her. She's not ready, Lord. She's not ready." He let out an anguished cry. He dropped to his knees beside the paramedic who was shaking his head at his partner. Tears were falling from his eyes, making everything seem blurry, unreal.

He watched the paramedic shake his head. They were pulling up a sheet over her, and he let his head drop into his hands. Sobbing, he cried out, "No. No. Please. Why!" so loud the men gathered around him fell silent.

"Buddy, you okay? Can we call someone for you?"

The paramedic was on his knees, trying to make eye contact with him.

He got up shaky but standing.

The paramedic took him by the arm and drew him over toward the police car. "Here, sit down for a minute. What's your name?"

Todd heard him yell for a water as if from a distance.

"Sir, I need to know if you can identify this lady? Sir?" he prompted politely.

One of the firemen handed him a bottle of water. "Here, drink this. It will help."

Todd took it unconsciously and swallowed a long pull of water. He was staring toward the wreck and shaking his head.

"Sir?"

Todd looked up at him blankly.

"Can you tell us her name?" he asked gently.

"It's Caroline. Was Caroline." He shuddered, letting the reality of that sink in. "She shouldn't be here. She's not supposed to be here."

"Sir, where should she be?"

Todd sighed, calming himself. "She lives in Seattle. She's my wife. Ex-wife," he amended quickly.

"You don't know what she was doing here?"

Todd shook his head no. "I guess she was coming to see me. We're trying to work out custody of our son."

The police officer wrote in his notebook and then took a step away. "Wait here a minute, okay? What's your name?"

"Todd. Todd Milner."

"Okay, Todd. You hold tight for a second. Do you want us to call anyone for you?"

*****

Hours later, Todd walked in the front door into Jenny's tight hug. He had phoned from the police station. She clung to him as he cried over Caroline. Tony, the officer who had taken his statement, told him sadly off the record that the alcohol level in Caroline's blood had been three times the legal limit. He couldn't understand what she was doing or why she was heading for him, and maybe he would never know. He was glad that Tony was calling her family. He didn't think he could have done it. They would blame him. Of that he was sure. Somehow her unhappiness, her drinking in their minds was his fault.

"Jen." It was a helpless cry.

She shhhed him softly, "It's okay, Todd. It's not your fault. It was never your fault."

He needed to hear that and was going to need to keep hearing it for some time.

"Laura said she is praying." Jenny had called her because she wanted to tell her what was going on but, more importantly, to have her pray for Todd, for Steve, for the fire, and now for this.

Todd looked up with a hopeful look. "She called? What did she say? Is she good?"

Laura—just the thought of her brought a calm to his spirit.

"I called her," Jen replied. "I wanted someone who would really pray."

Todd nodded in agreement. He was glad Jen had called.

"She said don't hesitate to call any time we need her."

"Thanks, Jen, for always being here for me. I know I don't always say so, but I couldn't do any of this without you."

"Same, Todd. We have to have each other's backs. That's what family is. That's what family does."

CHAPTER 24

. . . .

JENNY HEARD THE PHONE ring early in the morning and shot out of bed. Running down the stairs, she poked her head in the kitchen. Todd was already up and dressed and had made coffee.

He looked at her still quiet and moody but nothing like the day before.

"Hey, how ya doing?"

He shrugged. "Okay. Better, I think. I don't know." Shrugging, he sighed in resignation, "Look, I'm going to head into work. The wind is supposed to pick up today, and you know what that means. I want to get a jump on any stories, and I'll get you some news on Steve. I promise. Someone has to have information on him. I'm going to try and call Caroline's family today. I don't think it will go well. Keep praying for me, okay?" He headed out with a quick wave.

"I will!" Jen replied.

*****

Jenny was at the coffee shop that afternoon when she caught a broadcast from Todd.

This is Todd Milner for Ketchikan News Channel 12.

The Rolling Ridge fire which has raged here at the backdoor of Ketchikan for nearly two weeks now has dealt the firefighters yet another blow. Reports are coming in of a blow-up on the Eastern Ridge with firefighters allegedly trapped among the flames. We will be back with further updates. For Channel 12 news in Ketchikan, this is Todd Milner.

Jen pulled her phone out immediately and dialed Todd. "Hey, Jenny," he said wearily.

"Steve?"

"I don't know, Jen. The details are too sketchy. That's all I had, but Channel 12 wanted me to broadcast it."

"If you hear anything, will you please call?"

"I will. I promise. Pray, Jen. Don't forget to pray."

"I will. I love you, big brother."

"I love you too, lil sis."

She hung up the phone and took a deep breath and felt it at once: an urgent need to pray for Steve.

She flew to the backroom. "Maggie! Maggie!" Her voice was so agitated that Maggie came charging out of the office.

"What's wrong? Evacuation?" Maggie's face was etched with worry.

Jenny skidded to a stop in front of her. "Mags, I need a favor. I can't explain it, but I need to go. I need to do something. I'm really sorry, Mags, but can I go?"

As soon as Maggie nodded her head, Jenny was gone.

She flew home. She left Tyler at the sitters. She needed to be alone without distraction. She took the stairs two at a time and made it to her bedroom and hit her knees. She felt an urgency she had never felt before. She begged God to intercede, to keep Steve safe. "Oh, please, Father. You know what's happening, but I don't. I'm depending on You, Father God. Please, oh, please, help him."

CHAPTER 25

STEVE PAUSED IN HIS work. He was so tired. He could never remember being so tired. With the fire raging uncontrollably across most of the ridge, every available firefighter was out here trying to defend the towns from the deadly onslaught of flames.

Steve had spent much of the day in the sweltering heat, digging trenches and clearing brush with Ryan and Kevin. He could see Mike twenty yards behind them on the trail with his chainsaw. They were all sweating, panting, and continuously peeling the shirts from their bodies as they stuck sweat soaked to their skin.

It had to be 104 degrees. They had been at it for days, pounding into the dirt and touching off burnouts. It was Thursday now, and they had maybe gotten fourteen hours of sleep between them since Monday.

Steve could hear the shovels clanging, the chain saws screaming; he could see the guys ahead of him, heads down, elbows pumping, stealing the fuel from the fire to contain it.

They had gotten a report midafternoon when Steve had radioed, asking for another chainsaw and a trail grader to be included in the next drop. Over two hundred structures had been lost so far, and more than a dozen people were reported dead or injured. The winds were unpredictable, causing the flames to spread relentlessly onward. It seemed nothing they were doing was helping to turn the tide.

The flames kept advancing. Steve knew at this moment the chief was huddled around a map somewhere working out strategies. He prayed God would give him wisdom. They had gone into this fire season drier than ever before, and the thick black smoke hanging overhead marked the devastation.

Their crew had been dispatched to clear a broad path in the ridge, along the entire length of the three-mile ridge line. Bulldozers were moving the earth, and volunteers were out trimming or removing any brush in the fire path.

Two days ago, when the winds had shifted and began blowing from the south instead of the north, they had set a controlled fire of their own, hoping that the fire would hit the area they had cleared and have nowhere to go. Unfortunately, all that work had failed when the winds shifted again sending the fire down another path.

Overhead, Steve could see water planes and fire helicopters darting in and out of the billowing clouds of smoke trying to buy time for the guys like him on the ground—anything to slow the fire.

Steve hoped Jenny was okay. At least, she had Todd to watch out for her. He would be the first person to have any information or, at least, not long after the chief. That caused him to smile for the first time all day.

The smoke was getting thicker, and Steve could see the red glow of fire just past the ridgeline. It was too close. He shouldn't have run into it so soon. Kevin had directed them to spread out, but he must have moved off his coordinates in the gloom. He abandoned the shoveling and picked up his radio to call in. He was going to have to be more careful if he didn't want to get hurt and cause the team more problems by needing rescuing himself.

He clicked his radio to raise Mark at base camp. Nothing. He tried to raise Kevin. Nothing. He tried again and again with no luck. Equipment failure was not unheard of, but it was rare.

Steve took a minute to troubleshoot. He went over all his training, tried all the tricks. Nothing worked. He looked toward the ridge again and took a moment to decide on a course of action. His options were to go back and try to hook up with his team, but that meant a lot of backtracking, or he could move parallel to the fire in the hopes of exiting in the safety zone. He took another second and decided to move parallel to the fire.

He should run into Ryan and Kevin who were ahead of him. They could raise Mike, who was bringing up the rear on their radios and have him move forward to a new position. He hoisted his pack and secured his shovel with bungee cords, moving off at a brisk pace, watching the sky and the tops of the trees to get a sense of the fire's personality.

For a minute, he wondered what Jenny was doing. He missed her. It felt like he had been gone a year instead of two weeks.

*****

Jenny lost track of time. She could have been praying for minutes, or it could have been hours. She felt an urgent burden for Steve. She had knelt for a long time but now paced the room.

"Please, Lord," she said. "Please."

Once again, trying to surrender her will to God's. Once again, so afraid she might lose someone she could hardly breathe. She chose to believe by faith that the Lord was in charge of all things in her life. She would not go down the road of despair again.

She had learned too much about the Lord after her parents. She would not go through this without Him again.

God has plans to prosper me and do me no harm. God has my best interests at heart. God is my refuge in times of trouble. Jen encouraged herself, remembering a conversation she had with Laura. Laura had said something about how she would lean on her Creator and believe that He is good and that He does good for all His children no matter what the hardship she faced was.

She cried aloud in her room, "ABBA! Father," and suddenly felt His presence like she had never felt it before. He was with her, and just as suddenly, she knew He was with Steve, and He wanted her to know that. The burden lifted. She rose up off her floor and buried her head in her hands, sobbing in relief and joy. "Thank You, Lord," she whispered. "Thank You."

*****

Steve had lost them. The blowup had come with such intensity that there were branches circling over his head on updrafts, and a log had gone flying by close enough to scare him still. *Calm down. Breathe. You trained for this.* The smoke was now so thick he could hardly see to move forward.

In the gloom, he tripped over something; and looking down, he realized it was one of their chain saws. The sound of his heart pounded in his ears. If he thought things were bad before, he now realized things were desperate. For any of the crew to abandon their equipment was a last resort. It meant your life was in imminent danger. All that was left to do was run.

Steve ran.

It became a world where his thoughts consisted of repeating over and over in his mind. *Don't panic. Keep moving.* The fixation helped propel him forward for two miles hacking and coughing.

He stopped to wipe the grime out of his eyes and couldn't go any further. Exhausted, he fell to his knees and tried to hear over the roar of the fire.

For the first time, Steve ruefully admitted to himself that death was a very real possibility. *How do you handle it?* he thought and then realized just as quickly, you don't. It handles you. It rubs your nose in the reality that death comes to everyone, and there isn't a thing you can do about it.

His eyes filled with tears as he looked into his heart and realized that God was waiting for him, not so much to acknowledge death but to remind him that Jesus had conquered death. He didn't need to fear it. Not if he knew Him—the one who had conquered it.

Surrendering this journey was only a beginning. Here, he was a visitor, but home was heaven, and what was sweeter than home?

The tears were pouring down his face as a sob escaped from his lips, and finally understanding, he surrendered all. "Jesus, forgive me. Forgive my hesitation, my pride, my independence, my allegiance to a world that is filled with sin. Forgive me, Lord, and come into my heart. Take me now. I don't care. I know I'm coming home." He hesitated, looking up at the sky, which was glowing red like the fiercest sunset.

He wiped his face with the back of his hand, smearing the soot and grime and took a shallow breath, trying to get air. He spoke quietly from his heart to his creator, "But if it's possible, Lord, if it's Your will, give me a miracle here, Lord. I want to go back to Jen, Lord. I love her. I want to make her my wife. I want to be the kind of husband she deserves, a man of God. If You will, Lord, I thank You. But if not, I know that You know what's best for both of us. Help her, Lord. I think she loves me too, but she put You first, and I'm so grateful, Lord." He started crying again, "I'm so grateful for her. She helped me to see You first, and then all those other things will follow. I get it now, Lord. I hope it isn't too late."

He climbed wearily back to his feet. The fire was getting closer. There wasn't any way out. He nodded at God and began clearing the area around him of debris. He worked harder and faster than he ever had before. He didn't know where the strength came from, except from above.

He pulled the pouch off his waistband. No bigger than a box of chocolates, it was the one thing, *besides God*, that could save his life when everything else had gone wrong. It didn't look like it could do much of anything—a tiny aluminum foil pup tent. A floorless, frameless pop-up shelter bonded with an inner layer of heat resistant glass fiber able to withstand temperatures of 1,000 degrees.

Steve put his hands and feet in the straps and tucked the flap under him holding everything down with his elbows and knees, and he began to pray and worship God, and the peace that passed all understanding settled over him like a blanket as the roar of the fire engulfed him.

CHAPTER 26

THE SIRENS WENT OFF at noon. Jenny bolted from the bedroom and shot down the stairs. The phone rang as she skidded to a stop in the kitchen. "Hello."

"Jenny, it's Todd. Are you ready to go? I sent you a text, but I don't know if it went through. I heard the chief say they were going to evacuate. I'm already in the car. I'll be there in ten minutes."

"Okay." She took a deep breath. Wasn't that what she was supposed to do? Take deep calming breaths? At this rate, she was going to hyperventilate, and she didn't feel any calmer.

"Oh, Todd, you have to stop at Mary's and get Tyler. I was in a rush when I came home, and I didn't pick him up." Tears pooled in her eyes, but she blinked them back. No time to be a crybaby.

"Okay," he replied. "I'll grab him and honk the horn for you when I pull up."

Jen hung up the phone and looked at the duffel bag she had packed and put by the front door. She had their Bibles, some family pictures, Tyler's favorite toys and some clothes. *God, I hope this blows over. God, please give us a miracle.* "Steve, please, please, be alright," she whispered.

Jen watched from the front door as Todd sped up the driveway honking. He jumped out, and she followed his gaze to the sky behind the house. It glowed a deep reddish brown.

She closed and locked the front door behind her, looked up once more at the blazing sky, and shut her eyes, willing it to go away. All she could see was Steve surrounded by flames, and it was so real to her that she knew suddenly she was going to throw up. With a muffled cry, she stumbled to the side of the drive and emptied her stomach.

Todd jumped back out of the car and ran to her. "Oh, Jen, are you okay? Just hang on."

Bent over at the waist, she held up one hand and looked up with tears streaming down her face. "I'm okay," she said.

Todd handed her a tissue from his pocket. "Jen." The urgency came across in that one word.

She composed herself and headed for the car without another word.

Todd dropped Tyler and Jenny off at the front doors leading into the school, which was still filled with people who needed shelter. Jen got herself a cup of coffee and entertained Tyler so Todd could get some work done. However, when she hadn't seen him for more than an hour, she left Tyler in the childcare area to check on him.

He was silently praying in a corner. Placing her hand on his shoulder, she entered into prayer with him, agreeing for God to intervene and keep everyone safe. A commotion started on the other side of the room.

The first reports of the firefighters that were trapped on the ridge came in. It wasn't long before Todd and Jen heard three different versions of the story—all of them were bad. First, they heard that all the members of one hotshot team had died, causing Jen to momentarily lose her breath. Then a report that some had died, and some had survived.

"Todd," Jenn said urgently, "you need to find out what's happening. I can't." Jenn collapsed against the wall, hugging her knees into her chest. "I can't do it again, Todd. I can't."

"Come with me," Todd said, holding out a hand to help her up. "Let's head over to the chief and see if we can't get some straight answers."

Jenn nodded wearily and came to her feet. "Okay."

Todd asked to see the chief, who had snapped at everyone to back off and give him some space. His temper spoke volumes about the severity of the problem.

Jen and Todd inched their way toward the makeshift command center until they were in a good position to eavesdrop on the operation.

Chief yelled into a phone, the veins in his forehead prominently on display. Jenn felt sorry for whoever was on the receiving end of the line. "I don't care what he's doing! You get me that copter here now! We have four men down there, and they don't have twenty minutes! You get him back in there, you got it?" He slammed the phone down so hard that Jenn could hear the plastic crack.

Chief rubbed his bloodshot eyes and looked around at the people around the table. "Men, we need a miracle here. If you believe in God, now's the time to pray." He collapsed in a chair.

There was silence.

Jenn started to walk away. She didn't want to hear another word. As she turned away, a fireman came running up to the tent. "Chief, they've got them. Rescue team one picked them up a few minutes ago or, at least, three of them. Looks like the fourth got separated from the group. They're headed for the hospital and will do a flyby for the missing man."

Jenn was rooted to the spot.

The guy broke out in a smile as a cheer went up in the tent.

The chief shot out of his chair. "Get me their names. I want to know who's been found and who's still missing. I want to know what shape those men are in and what they can tell us about this fire. If one of those men can talk, I want him on the radio right now!"

No one moved.

"Waddya waiting for?" the chief roared. "Get moving!"

People shot out of the tent, sprinting off in every direction. The chief paced the tent like a caged lion. He looked up and caught Todd's eye.

Todd sprang to his feet and hurried over. Jen followed quickly behind him.

"Listen, Todd, hold on letting that out, will ya? I know there's gonna be lots of talk floating around, but these guys have families, and I don't want them thinking somebody's dead and gone when it might not be true. Might be we'll get lucky here, and everyone will make it out just fine. Ya get what I'm saying?"

Todd nodded quickly. "No problem, Chief. It's not my style to report on rumors anyway. I like my stuff based on facts."

"I knew I could count on you." The chief gave him a brief smile as he turned away.

Jenn nudged Todd.

"Chief," Todd said hesitantly.

The chief turned back with a raised eyebrow.

"One of the men, he's a friend. If you hear anything, could you let me know?"

The chief glanced from Todd to Jenny. "I'll take care of it, Todd. You'll be one of the first to know. And thanks again for sitting on this."

Todd nodded as he and Jenny walked back to the gym. "I have to give an update to the office. As soon as I hear something, I'll come find you here," Todd said, leaving her near the coffee table.

"There's Dawn. I'll go sit with her. Let me know the minute you hear something. If you can't come get me, just call my cell." Jenny looked at him and said, "The minute you hear something, Todd."

"Will do," Todd replied. He grabbed his computer bag and raced out of the gym.

*****

Jenny sat talking quietly with Dawn when her phone rang. "It's Todd," she stood abruptly, hitting accept. "Hey, Todd."

"Jenny, they found him."

She covered her mouth with her hand and shook her head.

"They found Steve. That's all I know. There's no word on whether or not he's okay."

"Steve," she whispered. Jenny sank slowly back down. "He's not dead?" Jenny asked.

Dawn watched her expectantly.

"Not that I know," Todd answered. "Jen, I need to get back to work. I'm going live soon. Are you going to be okay?"

"Go ahead. I'm fine. Dawn's with me. Let me know—"

"The minute I hear something," Todd finished for her. "I know, Jen."

Jen hung up the phone and looked at Dawn stricken. "They found him, but Todd doesn't know any more than that."

"Well, let's think positive. He's probably fine," Dawn replied.

"You really think so, Dawn?" Jenny said hopefully. "Wait, Dawn, do you hear that? It sounds like..."

They both looked up instinctively, realizing what it was. Jen scooped up Tyler and took off running for the door,

Dawn right behind her. A couple of other people headed out to see what the excitement was about.

Jen watched the rescue helicopter approaching from the east. It had to be the one. Jen couldn't tear her eyes off it. She watched it get closer, a bright spot in the drab gray sky as it passed over on the way to the hospital.

She could not be patient another minute. She had to know. She looked around frantically for Todd.

There! He stood next to the chief in the parking lot, taking notes. She pushed through the crowd. "Excuse me, Chief, I need to speak with Todd." Her tone was brisk. She was already tugging on his arm. She could see the concern etched on Dawn's face. She hadn't realized she was right next to her until she took Tyler out of her arms. She gave her a grateful smile and turned back to Todd. "I have to get to the hospital, Todd. I just need to, Todd. I need to be there for him. I need to know."

She wouldn't think about what she might find. Dead? Burned? She didn't want to imagine. She just wanted to know if her life had changed horribly and forever. Again.

"Do you want me to go with you?" he asked.

She shook her head. She remembered when her parents had died how she had clung to him.

"No. I need to face this alone. I can do this." She wasn't sure who needed the convincing more—her or him.

"I can do this," she repeated.

Fake it till you make it. She always thought that was a stupid phrase. Her mom used to say it endlessly. Now she got it. It was about hanging on for dear life so you wouldn't fall down or break down.

She was in the car when her phone started to ring. It was Dawn. "I just wanted to see if you were really okay. You okay?" Worry laced her voice.

"Oh, Dawn." Her voice shook despite her best efforts to keep it steady. She sniffed. "I'm not sure what I'm going to find, but I have to know if he's…" she couldn't say it. "I have to know if he's okay," she said lamely.

"Oh, sweetie, I'm so sorry. I didn't realize it was like that. I mean, I knew you liked him and all, and here I teased you. Oh my gosh, I feel terrible." Dawn was crying now, so, of course, Jenny started crying.

"I know. It's okay." She wiped the tears. "Look, I'd better get off this phone before I run off the road. I'm okay, really." She was okay. She felt it.

God was near her. She knew without a shadow of a doubt that she was in a far different place now than when her parents died. She was stronger in her faith and surer of God's omnipotent hand, His unfailing grace. She would not blame God; she would only seek and receive His comfort.

With more strength than she ever imagined, she made her way to the hospital parking lot, parked the car, and walked up through the emergency room doors. Taking a deep breath, she approached the receptionist.

*****

The woman hung up the phone she was on and looked up seeming a bit harried. "May I help you?" she asked wearily.

"I'm looking for the firefighter that just came in. Steve Baltyn. He…he… I—" Jen forced herself to stop. She could tell the nurse was overwhelmed. The nurse didn't even ask if she was family, just quickly wrote a room number down on a post it and shoved it across the desk while waving in the general direction of the room as she picked up the ringing phone. "Nurses' station, Caitlin speaking, how can I help you?"

Jen didn't give her a chance to change her mind and sped off down the hallway in the direction the nurse had indicated.

She found Steve's room and went in. He was asleep. She settled in the chair next to the bed and studied him. There were smudges of dirt on his nose and forehead. He looked like a five-year-old just in from playing outside. The hair on his arm was singed; his eyebrows all but gone, but other than that, he didn't look like he had suffered any injuries.

Jenny gulped and looked up at the ceiling, trying to make the tears stop. Hopeless. It was too much to ask she supposed, considering Hallmark commercials made her sob and those animal shelter commercials? As soon as the music came on and the first abused dog appeared, she had to change the channel. She sighed and touched Steve's cheek, wondering at the miracle that he was alive and well.

He started to stir, and she snatched her hand back as he opened his eyes. He blinked at her, and she smiled. He was adorable.

"Hi," she whispered.

"Jenny?"

"Yup. It's me. In the flesh." Her smile wavered, and her eyes filled up again. She swiped at the tears, embarrassed. "You scared the life out of us!" She tried to scold him, but her quivering voice gave her away. "What happened?"

He kept smiling at her with a look in his eyes that made her glad she was sitting down.

"I'm sorry, Jenny. To tell you the truth, I'm not sure what happened. I got separated from the team, and—" He closed his eyes and shrugged. "I don't know. I can't remember. Did anyone—are the guys okay?"

"Oh, I'm sorry. Yes, everyone is fine! I didn't think to tell you right away. I'm so sorry. I was so worried about you."

She looked away, embarrassed by the longing in her voice. She felt her face growing hot.

Steve smiled a sappy smile at her again, and she couldn't help but smile back.

"Jenny, I have something to tell you." He reached over and took her hand.

She inhaled sharply and reminded herself to be calm.

"When things looked pretty hopeless out there, I realized something. Well, two things." He caught her eyes and held them. "I realized that the Lord loved me, and I surrendered everything to Him."

She was speechless, her joy bubbling to the surface.

"And I realized," he paused, looking at her intently, "I love you."

Jenny stopped breathing; she was sure she was hearing things. She concentrated on Steve's lips.

He had really soft looking lips.

She shook her head to clear it. "I'm sorry, Steve, what did you say?"

He let out a booming laugh. "Jen, did you hear a word I just said? You big goof. I love you. I. Want. To. Marry. You." He drew it out as if she was a simpleton as he continued to laugh.

"What are you thinking about in that head of yours? No, wait, don't tell me. I don't even want to know."

"I love you. Do you love me?"

She was so stunned; all she could do was nod yes.

"Will you marry me?"

She nodded again, and he let out a whoop and pulled her into his arms.

A smile broke out on her face.

"I love you, Jenny."

She snuggled into his arms.

"I love you too, Steve. I do. I love you." She enjoyed being in his arms. She enjoyed saying how she felt out loud.

When he lifted her chin, she closed her eyes, feeling his lips soft against her own. She was breathless when he stopped, and she buried her face in his chest. His arms went around her, and they both contentedly sighed.

"We're getting married soon," he said, matter of fact, "before another fire starts."

"Absolutely," she replied just as matter of fact.

THE END

In the second heartwarming story of the series, *Dawn*, Jenny is planning her wedding, Todd is considering a network offer, and Dawn is battling her own personal demons. Join me for a cup of coffee at Maggie's as we continue with life in Ketchikan.

CPSIA information can be obtained
at www.ICGtesting.com
Printed in the USA
LVHW022350020920
664821LV00002B/135